An Introduction to Administration for Social Workers

First Published in 1967, *An Introduction to Administration for Social Workers* argues that the tasks of social workers in our society cannot be understood without considering the administrative framework within which they work- a new approach requiring much study and research. In this book Joyce Warham examines some of its most important aspects.

The book progresses from the theoretical to the practical. Part I presents a background of theories of organization and of management, stressing elements generic to all organizations, and with the object of offering a 'frame of reference' for considering the nature of administration. Part II begins with a discussion of the characteristics of social work agencies as distinct from organizations of other kinds and moves on from there to consider the specific function and tasks of the administrator. This is an important introductory volume for students of social work.

I0105080

An Introduction to Administration for Social Workers

Joyce Warham

Routledge
Taylor & Francis Group

First published in 1967
by Routledge & Kegan Paul Ltd.

This edition first published in 2024 by Routledge
4 Park Square, Milton Park, Abingdon, Oxon, OX14 4RN

and by Routledge
605 Third Avenue, New York, NY 10017

Routledge is an imprint of the Taylor & Francis Group, an informa business

© Joyce Warham 1967

Publisher's Note
The publisher has gone to great lengths to ensure the quality of this reprint but points out that some imperfections in the original copies may be apparent.

Disclaimer
The publisher has made every effort to trace copyright holders and welcomes correspondence from those they have been unable to contact.

A Library of Congress record exists under LCCN: 67073656

ISBN: 978-1-032-90273-9 (hbk)
ISBN: 978-1-003-54686-3 (ebk)
ISBN: 978-1-032-90276-0 (pbk)

Book DOI 10.4324/9781003546863

An Introduction to Administration for Social Workers

by Joyce Warham

Lecturer in Sociology, University of Keele

LONDON

ROUTLEDGE AND KEGAN PAUL

NEW YORK: THE HUMANITIES PRESS

First published 1967
by Routledge and Kegan Paul Ltd
Broadway House, 68-74 Carter Lane
London, E.C.4

Reprinted 1970

Printed in Great Britain
by Redwood Press Limited
Trowbridge and London

© Joyce Warham 1967

SBN 7100 3947   6   (p)
SBN 7100 3941   7   (c)

General editor's introduction

The Library of Social Work is designed to meet the needs of students following courses of training for social work. In recent years the number and kinds of training in Britain have increased in an unprecedented way. But there has been no corresponding increase in the supply of text-books to cover the growing differentiation of subject matter or to respond to the growing spirit of enthusiastic but critical enquiry into the range of subjects relevant to social work. The Library will consist of short texts designed to introduce the student to the main features of each topic of enquiry, to the significant theoretical contributions so far made to its understanding, and to some of the outstanding problems. Each volume will suggest ways in which the student might continue his work by further reading.

Social work and the social agency in which it is practised are in many important ways inseparable, in spite of the development in American social work of so-called private practice. Recently, social workers have come to see the collaboration and conflict of worker, client and agency as an important dynamic process. Joyce Warham shows how far our interest in social work has progressed since the early concern with office efficiency, and how much more complex and stimulating the study of social work administration is than the simple recounting of the detail of relevant social legislation.

This book outlines an approach which is still at an exploratory stage. It is one of a number devoted to problems and issues in social work of a general character, bringing together in an illuminating way theoretical ideas and a firm grasp of the concrete problems of social work practice. Others in this series include professionalism in social work, and ethics and social work. The study of administrative processes and roles is certainly one of the growing points in contemporary social work.   NOEL TIMMS

Contents

Introduction

'In our agencies, administration tends to be viewed simply as a necessary part of bureaucratic structure which, at best, is tolerated with a poor grace. Rarely is it seen as a creative process, and as an integral part of social work practice' (Gold, B. H., unpublished paper read to National Conference on Social Welfare, Los Angeles, 1964).

This assertion about American social service agencies seems to ring true to the situation in this country also. Whether 'the administration' be conceived as the Home Office, requiring that Probation Officers fill in certain forms at certain times, or as the complex organisational hierarchy of a large hospital, or as the lay, as distinct from the professional social work staff of a Children's Department, it tends to be looked on as something which functions in a separate world from social work. When it impinges on social work, it is felt as restricting the worker's freedom to do his professional job. It is as if the social worker would, if he could, immerse himself in some mythical activity called 'pure casework', and leave administration to 'them'.

If this indeed is the predominant feeling, why should it be so? Is it because the activities we think of as administrative are unhelpful to social work? Or because administrators are insufficiently knowledgeable about, and committed to, social work objectives and methods? Or because social work training focuses on teaching students to use themselves as individuals rather than to work as members of organisations? Or because organisations tend to become ends in themselves, with administration serving the organisation itself, rather than the purpose for which it was established?

These are some of the questions which seem to demand attention if a more positive role for, and attitude to, administration is to develop. The basic assumption of this monograph is that administration is a method by which a conscious attempt can be made to ensure that in every respect possible, an organisation is geared effectively to the work it has to do. If, for example, the primary purpose of a factory is to make a profit, and that of a hospital to treat the sick, and that of a social work agency to give a social work service to clients, then it is the function of industrial management, and of hospital or social work administration, to create an organisation which will be the most effective instrument possible for achieving these ends.

This does not mean that a wholly effective or tension-free working unit can be achieved, by even the most skilled or committed social work administrator; for it is a factor to be reckoned with that many of the conflicts between social work and administration may be inherent in the very nature of organisations themselves. The bureaucratic culture, for example, calls for loyalty to the organisation, while the professional culture has its roots in professional standards and affiliations. However professionally concerned he may be, the administrative head of an agency has a different perspective from that of the social worker, and will tend to identify with the needs of the organisation in its entirety as well as, it is hoped, with the purposes of social work. And even the social worker himself, although loth to do so, may need to 'understand and accept that the social worker's professional self is in practice probably as much a function of social work's bureaucratic mode of organisation, as it is a function of the formally stated ideals of the profession' (Morgan, 1962). For example, such associations as the National Association of Probation Officers and the Association of Child Care Officers do not so much represent professional social work, as reflect the impact of social service structure on professional organisation. Indeed one of the characteristics of professional organisations seems to be the bureaucratic one of self-preservation.

That one function of any organisation is self-maintenance is a sociological truth which has to be faced; and that social work is dependent on organisations is another. Unless we can check the tendency of organisations to become 'ends in themselves', we must reckon with the sort of danger confronted by social services for children:

> There is a real danger that the growing complexity and specialisation of these services will make it increasingly hard for social workers to give effective help to the people they serve, and increasingly easy for them to become mere instruments of the administration (Donnison, 1958).

The wish to minimise such a danger will be ineffective unless allied to the means. One appropriate instrument may be social action, aimed at legislative reform; another the professional conscience of social workers and their sense of personal responsibility to clients; and yet another, the kind of administration which while recognising the tensions between organisational demands and restraints on the one hand, and the preserves of professional competence and discretion on the other, is primarily committed to the social work function of the agency.

In broad outline, the administrative structure of the statutory social services is laid down in legislation and, on a short term basis at least, must be taken as given: we cannot 'shatter it to bits, and then remould it nearer to the heart's desire'. And it is not only the broad structure which has to be accepted: Boarding-out Regulations, Adoption Rules, Approved School Rules, Probation Rules, and so on, are all expressions of the degree of control which is exercised by statutory means over those whom the community employs to implement its social policy. The latitude for action available to the head of a statutory agency is limited by factors which he may have to accept because he is powerless to change them. But this apart, his freedom is determined in practice by his capacity to distinguish realistically between situations which have to be accepted because they cannot be changed, and those in which change is both possible and desirable. Even this however is a complex business, for improvement is possible provided only 'that we can agree on what really constitutes an improvement' (Lippitt, 1958).

There is perhaps a parallel with social work itself: for as the social worker seeks to understand the nature of the client's situation, and to work with and within the possibilities it offers, so those who carry administrative responsibility within an agency may also, by a process involving the relating of means to ends, have a 'problem-solving' and an 'enabling' contribution to make.

This argument, however, presupposes that there exists a body of knowledge about the nature of organisations, and ways of managing them, upon which it is possible to draw. One of the dilemmas of applied social science is that it is extensively based on hypotheses which for a time hold the

4

field, and then are superseded. The theorist is free to pursue truth indefinitely, but the social worker cannot wait until the causes of, for example, maladjustment or delinquency are 'known'. He must act, even although both the knowledge available to him, and his own interpretation of it, are of necessity imperfect. So it is for the administrator. Nevertheless, in both organisation theory, and in theories of management, there is a developing body of knowledge available to him, as sociology, psychology, and casework theory are available to the social worker.

That this is so, is generally accepted in formal training for management in industry. A post-graduate Personnel Management course, for example, is concerned basically with the application of social science knowledge to the role and functions of the personnel manager, within the context of the factory. A social service agency has characteristics which distinguish it from other types of organisation, and theories of organisation and of management will be relevant only if their application allows for these. This said, however, might not social work administration, like industrial management, profitably draw on current thinking on such topics as, to give random examples, the characteristics of the working group, problems of communication, organisations as both formal structures and 'social systems', and the nature of authority?

If this is so, the question arises as to who in the agency is to put such knowledge to use: who *is* the administrator? A typical structural division in a Children's Department is the tripartite one of 'administration', Child Care staff, and residential staff; and in all agencies the tendency may be to regard any member of staff who is not a social worker as being part of 'the administration'. But this is a false division. Overall responsibility for the agency is vested in the person who holds the position of agency head, be he

Children's Officer, or Family Service Unit Leader, or the Senior Medical Social Worker of a hospital Social Service department. His role is clearly an administrative one; but what of the social work member of staff? He controls some of the agency's resources, in the form of his own skills, and through the use he makes of clerical skills; he must share the agency's resources with colleagues; and as an employee he is accountable to the agency for the use of his time. He has, to sum up, the *administrative* responsibility of deploying the resources he controls, not in relation to his own needs alone, but in the service of the agency. Every social worker *is* an administrator, performing his social work role not in isolation, but in a working situation in which his effectiveness depends on the co-ordination of his activities with those of others. And what of the clerk or telephonist? Those whose work we are inclined to regard as administrative in the 'paperwork' sense are also full members of social work agencies; and the way in which the telephonist handles an enquiry, may be the deciding factor in a prospective client's decision whether or not to keep an appointment with a social worker.

And so, it is suggested, administration is not something altogether separable from social work; and 'the administration' is not separate from the rest of the agency. This introductory text is thus not addressed exclusively to those members of agencies who carry no caseloads. The focus will be on those positions in which the administrative as distinct from the social work practice element is dominant, but an attempt will be made continuously to relate the two. Whatever of interest there may be for those who hold positions of administrative responsibility, or who see their future careers as lying in this field, it is believed also that an understanding of the structure and functioning of the organisation of which they are a part, may help practising social workers to clarify their own roles within it, not only as social workers, but also as colleagues and as employees.

In broad outline, the monograph progresses from the theoretical to the practical. Part I presents a background of theories of organisation and of management, stressing elements generic to all organisations, and with the object of offering a 'frame of reference' for considering the nature of administration. Part II begins with a discussion of the characteristics of social work agencies as distinct from organisations of other kinds, and moves on from there to consider the specific function and tasks of the administrator. Readers with a social science background will, it is hoped, like Alice in Wonderland find it sensible to begin at the beginning, and go straight on. But an alternative approach might be a preliminary reading of chapters V and VI.

PART ONE

A theoretical background

I

The origins of modern management

Organisations have always required to be administered – whether by rule of thumb, or in accordance with an elaborately codified set of instructions as in Queen's Regulations. Of recent years there have become available theories of management on which administrators can draw, and latterly these have increasingly been derived from theories about the nature of organisations. During the seventy years or so during which theories of management have been developing, there have been major changes in emphasis; and at this point in time, the wise approach for those who would draw on the now extensive literature in an attempt to evolve a more rational basis for their own practice, would seem to be an eclectic one.

This and the next two chapters will present, in very broad outline, some theories about organisations and management, as a preliminary to the subsequent discussion of administration in social work agencies. Some justification needs first perhaps to be offered for a theoretical approach to what is customarily regarded as an essentially 'practical' activity.

In general, theory is relevant to practice if it contributes to the more accurate diagnosis of the situation under review, helps to increase the range of alternatives from which a choice of action can be made, gives a wider perspective on the implications of particular lines of action, and provides a frame of reference within which diverse activities can be co-ordinated, and a sense of direction be developed. In respect of all this, one of the attributes of a professional person is his capacity to draw on theoretical knowledge:

> The professional draws upon the knowledge of science and of his colleagues, and upon knowledge gained thrcugh personal experience. The degree to which he relies upon the first two of these, rather than the third, is one of the ways in which the professional may be distinguished from the layman. (McGregor, 1960)

In social work, such an approach to theory is familiar, for the social worker is continuously concerned with the application of social science knowledge to the service of individual clients. Much of this process becomes so automatic that it operates almost unconsciously. So familiar is the social worker with the concept of maternal deprivation for example, that the undesirability of separating a child unnecessarily from his mother is taken for granted, and what is owed to the theoretical work of Dr. Bowlby may not cross the social worker's mind. But the theory is nevertheless fundamentally affecting his practice; and to the extent that he is interested in his own professional development, he will not only be drawing on the theoretical knowledge he already has, but seeking also to expand it.

This stage in the application of theoretical knowledge is obviously far from being reached in the administration of social work agencies. Of all the factors influencing the situation, one is that such knowledge has not been made accessible, through formal training, to those who carry administrative responsibility. Furthermore, although professional social workers have now for long regarded psychology and sociology as disciplines useful for the advancement of their social work skills, they have not looked to similar sources to enhance their administrative skills, or their understanding of the nature of their working environment. There is thus as yet comparatively little in the way of a literature on administration specifically applied to social work agencies, but the following necessarily brief presentation of a theoretical background will, it is hoped, indicate that there is a harvest to be reaped here too.

I. A SCIENCE OF MANAGEMENT

An early advocate of a rational approach to management was Robert Owen (1771–1858), whose argument remains pertinent:

> If due care as to the state of your inanimate machines can produce such beneficial results, what may not be expected if you devote equal attention to your vital machines, which are far more wonderfully constructed. (Owen, 1813)

But pertinent though the suggestion may be, it is perhaps ethically open to question: do men matter because they are instruments of production, or because they are men? The dilemma is one which administrators of social work agencies, which produce services and not goods, may find it easier to resolve than has industry. But it is to industry nevertheless that we must turn for much of the pioneer thinking about methods of management; for it is only very recently indeed that social work in this country has begun to turn its attention to such matters.

In the industrial field already before the turn of the century there had begun an attempt to synthesise thinking about management. The outstanding pioneer was the American F. W. Taylor (1856–1915), who in 1895 published a paper suggesting the possibility of a scientific approach to the study of management. It was Taylor who laid the foundations on which all subsequent work in this field in Great Britain has been based. His ambition was to substitute 'exact scientific investigation and knowledge for the old individual judgment or opinion' (Urwick, 1951) in the organisation of industrial undertakings, and particularly in securing maximum output. Taylor was a brilliant engineer, and his basic method was to apply the techniques of engineering to organisation. The role he identified for 'exact scientific knowledge' has a nineteenth century ring about it, and one perhaps finds more congenial the view that 'it is precisely our uncertainty which brings us a good deal closer to reality than was possible in former periods which had faith in the absolute' (Mannheim, 1954). Nevertheless, Taylor and other pioneers, in their attempts to apply reason and intelligence to organisational problems, gave an identity to the concept of management, and provided it with a rationale: Taylor was doing for management what Mary Richmond (1917) was doing for casework.

Out of this disciplined approach emerged the method which came to be known as 'scientific management'. This derived from essentially negative assumptions about the behaviour of employees, and from a basically authoritarian attitude to the use of power. But it had its idealistic aspects too, and its adherents saw 'in its principles of detachment, of objectivity, of measurement, not only greater prosperity for the community, but a way of escape from the self-regarding struggles of groups or classes which hag-ride our machine economy' (Urwick, 1951).

In broad terms, the 'scientific managers' assumed that the worker was lazy and needed to be prodded. He was untrustworthy and his judgment was limited, so he needed to be controlled. He was not interested in the prosperity of the organisation, but was completely egocentric; and his attitudes were largely unmodifiable. It was on this concept of the rank and file employee that the model of 'scientific management' was based. Control imposed from above was seen as the most effective method of getting work done, and of integrating diverse operations. The organisation appeared as a pyramid of super-subordinate positions, with individuals functioning under the orders of those above them in the hierarchy. Decisions relating to major change were to originate from the top; and the flow of communication, which was downwards, served primarily for the transmission of orders. At the lowest step on the hierarchy, supervision was directed to 'overseeing', rather than to the development of the capacity of the worker as an individual. The interests of the 'scientific managers' were in the development of increasingly precise methods of control: order, efficiency, precision, were key words.

To anyone reared in the democratic climate of mid-twentieth century social work, and equipped with any knowledge of psychological theory, such an approach to management must seem both an affront to human dignity, and unlikely to succeed. But two major points must be made before we dismiss 'scientific management' as of exclusively historical interest.

Firstly, it established very firmly the idea that management was a process which demanded an intellectual approach, and it aimed at evolving a rational basis on which

15

'management' and 'men' could co-operate in maximising efficiency. With the wisdom of hindsight we can now criticise the 'scientific managers' for shortcomings in their understanding of human motivation, but to them is due the credit for demonstrating that methods of management can be evolved in the light of advancing knowledge in the social sciences. And this principle holds good today.

Secondly, although 'scientific management' in the form in which Taylor propounded it may no longer have its formal adherents, its influence is still pervasive. Time and Motion Study, and 'Organisation and Method', are its direct descendants; and the resistance to the idea of supervision so widely displayed by social workers in this country may still owe a great deal to the connotations of 'overseeing' acquired by the term 'supervision' via industrial management. But above all the idea of management by imposed control may still insidiously touch a chord of authoritarianism in all those who carry administrative responsibility. It is a tidy approach : it has affinities with the formal structure of large organisations; and its premises once accepted, its logic may appeal to the orderly minded.

2. WORKERS AS HUMAN BEINGS

'Scientific management' attached overriding importance to the organisation itself, at the expense of those employed in it. That the emphasis shifted was in no small degree due to the work of one woman. The interests of Mary Follett (1865?–1933) ranged far beyond business administration. Trained as a political scientist, she earned for herself a considerable reputation in that field, but was also for long active in social work in her native Boston – in a Settlement, in Evening Education Centres, and in Vocational Guidance. It is to her contribution to the development of what is perhaps best described as a 'philosophy' of administration that we must confine ourselves here. Her papers on this subject have a rare inspirational quality, combined with a psychological and practical sophistication which still astonishes thirty years after her death. If social workers think of administration as arid, they might well turn to her for refreshment.

Miss Follett's ties with England were close, and it was to English industrialists that the majority of her papers on administration were presented. Her primary interest was in the psychological factors which operate within any organisation, and in the relationships between individuals, and within groups, in the process of management. For the earlier 'scientific managers', management was a static concept: Mary Follett saw it as dynamic. Major significance is given to the individual, and to the groups of which he feels himself to be a part; conflict (or difference, as Miss Follett preferred to see it) is looked on as essential to growth, and as demanding resolution rather than repression; the problem of giving orders leads her 'into the heart of the whole question of authority and consent' (Metcalf, 1941); and power is seen as a correlate of responsibility. Conflict and integration, the individual and the group, power and responsibility, consent and participation, are representative concepts in Mary Follett's theory of administration as a method of promoting the co-operation which is necessary for getting work done. Her essentially pragmatic approach is founded on sensitivity to the feelings of the individual, and on respect for human worth and personal dignity; psychology replaces engineering as the source material for management theory; and the way begins to open for the development of thinking about management primarily in terms of human relations.

During the first world war, attention began to focus on

17

the effect of physical working conditions on output. By the mid-twenties, the Western Electric company, engaged at its Hawthorne plant on research into the effect of lighting on production, was forced to recognise that the validity of a carefully controlled scientific experiment was being nullified by a failure to identify and isolate the modifying effect of the 'human element'. In sum, the crucial factors affecting production appeared to be human rather than physical. From then on, the 'Hawthorne Investigations' focussed on the study of workers as individuals and, particularly, as members of groups. Of this massive and lengthy undertaking, a major by-product in the nineteen-thirties was the emergence of theories of management in terms of social relationships: the psychological acuity of Mary Follett found itself justified in the light of empirical research.

In Roethlisberger's *Management and Morale* (1955) one finds an interpretation of the Hawthorne research, and a presentation of the emergent philosophy of management. The book reveals the extent to which by 1940 management theory was drawing on philosophy, social anthropology, sociology, and psychology; all of them source material for social work also. Roethlisberger is concerned to analyse the social structure of industry, and to identify the function of management within it. This function he sees primarily in terms of enhancing 'human collaboration', and some of the questions he poses in relation to this may indicate his approach.

These relate basically to the relationship between men, work, and organisation. What does the individual bring with him to the employment situation? What does the situation demand of him? What are the formal patterns of behaviour in a group? And the informal ones? How can balance be maintained between interacting forces such as these? What skills does the administrator use in attempting to achieve such equilibrium? And can such skills be explicitly formulated?

As with the 'scientific managers', the 'control' element is foremost. But it is a different kind of control, which does not derive simply from authority assumed from position in the hierarchy: 'Effective human control can be exercised by a person in a position of responsibility *only through an adequate understanding of the human situations he is administering*' (Roethlisberger, 1955). The organisation itself is no longer to be described simply in terms of a formal hierarchy, for it is composed of 'human situations' also. 'Dynamic situations involving the interaction of people' are for Roethlisberger perhaps the major component of any organisation, and from him we have the germ of the idea to be explored by later theorists: the organisation as a social system.

What has come to be known as the 'human relations' school dominated management theory well into the nineteen fifties. It emphasised the *unplanned* aspects of organisational behaviour – the emotional elements in motivation, for example, and in particular the influence of informal social groupings. To it we owe the concept of the *informal organisation*, functioning alongside and impinging upon the formal structure shown on an organisation chart. Who is the 'real' leader in the workshop? Is it the foreman, or alternatively someone with no 'formal' authority at all? Why may people resist transfer to a job carrying the apparent attractions of better pay and working conditions? These are the kind of questions which the 'human relations' school posed and explored, in their attempt to integrate the 'human factor' into the very process of management itself.

The excitement of the breakaway from the static and authoritarian concepts of the 'scientific managers' is still to be felt throughout the literature. The 'human relations' school postulated an optimistic view of management, in which greater personal satisfaction for the worker and increased productivity were to complement each other. The difficulties were not minimised; for the objective was 'good human relations' not through the erratic instrument of intuition, but soundly based on a hard-won body of communicable knowledge. 'All problems of human relationship, whether in industry or elsewhere, are complex, and the earliest study must therefore be clinical,' wrote the founding-father Elton Mayo (1946).

The overriding importance attached to the understanding of human behaviour, and to the recognition by management that its primary concern is with people, is surely congenial to social workers. If it now also sounds obvious, it is perhaps relevant to recall that the 'human relations' contribution to management theory was made at a time when the almost unquestioned basis for management was imposed control; that the authoritarian and intuitive approaches are still both widespread and tenacious; and that professional social work itself has hardly begun to relate to agency administration that knowledge of the behavioural sciences upon which it draws in working with clients.

3. THE ORGANISATION AND ITS TASK

Of lasting significance for the impetus it gave to the scientific study of human behaviour within organisations, the 'human relations' school yet made in common with 'scientific management' a major assumption which must now be called in question : that there was no ineradicable conflict between the needs of the individual and those of the organisation, and that the satisfaction of the one was reconcilable with the efficiency of the other. The 'scientific managers' saw the worker as motivated by economic factors, and responding to the efficiency which would increase his income; and the 'human relations' school claimed that through democratic management, the organisation could meet the social needs of the worker, increase his co-operation, and by making him 'happy' make him also productive.

Underlying this assumption was the implicit one that management and workers have a common goal: the success of the organisation. But the 'human relations' view, as the 'scientific management' view before it, was essentially partisan – a *management* oriented view. There was a dilemma implicit in its pursuit of satisfaction for the worker as an agent of production; it failed to reckon with the highly institutionalised character of labour/management conflict. Against its contribution to the exploration of ways of minimising conflict, is to be set its failure to recognise that there may be situations in which, because the interests of participating groups are irreconcilable, conflict is itself inherent. The problem is succinctly posed by Etzioni (1964): 'A point is reached in every organisation where happiness and efficiency cease to support each other. Not all work can be well paid or gratifying, and not all regulations and orders can be made acceptable. Here we face a true dilemma.'

If this is indeed so, then a new dimension affects the role of management: 'good human relations' are not exclusively a function of the interaction between management and men, but have to be sought within the boundaries of the demands imposed by the organisation itself. The conditions and limitation imposed by the purpose for which all the employees of an organisation are brought together, and indeed by the very nature of the work to be done, emerge as factors which inexorably affect the ways in which, and the extent to which, tension can be relieved. Without carrying the analogy too far, it is possible to suggest a comparison with social work. The worker/client relationship also has its boundaries, which include both the functions of the agency employing the worker, and the nature of the social work task to be done: and the limitations and opportunities which the social worker finds in the 'setting' will have a counterpart for management, whose 'primary setting' is the organisation.

Fundamentally different though the 'scientific management' and 'human relations' schools in many ways were, they were yet both identified with the 'management side' of industry. A subsequent approach has been to subject to rigorous scrutiny the nature of organisations themselves – the settings in which management is practised, and of which it is itself an integral part.

The 'structuralists' are social scientists investigating social phenomena, untrammelled by allegiances to management, or by a philosophy of worker/management relations. Their concern is not the promotion of efficiency, but rather the objective analysis of organisations. To illustrate this approach, one might take the example of conflict. For the 'human relations' school, conflict was ideologically abhorrent, and therefore to be minimised; for the 'structuralist' it is in itself neither good nor bad, but a social fact to be studied, and of which the causes – and the functions – are to be sought both within the structure of the organisation itself, and in the interaction between the organisation and the environment in which it functions.

The field of study now widens, and it becomes possible to see more clearly the relevance of organisation theory to organisations of any kind – including social work agencies. Both 'scientific management' and the 'human relations' school focussed on industry: but the 'structuralists' are interested in organisations irrespective of kind. One writer, for example, explores the characteristics of the mental hospital – of the 'total institution' which cuts its inmates off from intercourse with the outside world (Goffman, 1961). His thesis is that the mental hospital patient is 'formed' by the hospital in which he finds himself, rather than by his illness; and although the impact of the organisation upon the individual is accentuated in this type of organisation, the nature of the relationship between an organisation and the individuals within it is of universal significance, whether the organisation be a prison, or a probation department, or a university. Another study (Gouldner, 1955) investigates the relationship between a factory and the community in which it is located, and the ways in which the norms and values of that community are brought into the factory, and affect its very structure; and yet another (Blau, 1963) analyses the impact of bureaucratic structure on inter-personal relations in civil service settings.

Empirical studies such as these represent an attempt to clarify 'what goes on' in organisations, and are to be seen against the background of the search for a conceptual frame of reference which has engrossed theorists from Weber onwards. The point to be noted here is the *generic* quality of concepts such as bureaucracy, communication, authority and responsibility. As concepts, they are relevant to organisations of whatever kind. Both empirically and theoretically, perhaps one of the most significant developments of the 'post human-relations period', from the point of view of social work administration, has been the shift in focus from the factory to the *'organisation'*.

In this very broad outline of some of the major developments in management and organisation theory, it remains to indicate what is now emerging as a potentially more rational foundation for effective management than either the authoritarian control of the 'scientific managers', or the free-floating 'human relations' approach. The first saw the employee exclusively as an instrument of production; the second, while recognising the existence of his social and psychological needs, yet failed to identify those factors in the employment situation which meant that, with the best will in the world, those needs could not all be met. Theoretical insight into the characteristics of organisations, and empirical studies of the factors which determine the ways in which they function, called for a new approach. A synthesis is found in focussing on the *task* – the work which the organisation has to do in order to remain in existence. In the 'task' approach to management, 'both instruments and people are considered, *but in relation to the work that has to be done*' (Brown, 1960). Yet another parallel may be drawn with social work: for as the social worker must be clear about the social work purpose of the worker/client relationships, so the 'task' theory of management calls for the clear identification of agency purposes, and the mobilisation of resources in relation to them.

Social workers as such have to make use of organisations, and are continually assessing their capacity to meet the needs of clients. They are familiar with the concept of the 'informal' life of the prison, which meets social needs which the formal structure fails to meet; they are aware of ways in which organisations such as Approved Schools and Detention Centres appear ill-contrived in relation to their declared purposes; and in the Child Care field, experiments with purpose-built Homes represent a search for that type of organisational setting most appropriate to the declared purpose of compensating children for the lack of a normal home life.

But social work agencies are themselves *organisations,*

and as such may be analysed in relation to their purposes. They have characteristics which they share with all formal organisations, as well as some which are special to them, and demand some specialisation in administration. The next chapter will present some concepts which seem to offer particular insight into the nature of organisations – which are both the administrator's setting, and also his 'raw material'.

II

The nature of organisations

The organisation has been referred to as the administrator's 'raw material'. It might also be described as an instrument which he can use in working towards objectives. All this implies that any organisation has an identity which can be described and analysed, and that it can in some measure at least be consciously controlled, and shaped into a form appropriate to given purposes. It also implies that the administrator himself sees the organisation as being malleable: that is, to paraphrase Bagehot, that he sees it not as something finished and complete – 'a grand and achieved result' – but rather as a 'working and changeable instrument'.

If this instrument is to be effectively used, its potentialities and limitations need to be understood. This chapter will attempt to indicate some theoretical concepts which seem to have particular relevance in this respect. The administrator may learn through experience, as may the untrained social worker; but it is also open to him to draw on what has already been learned by others. 'Although theory without practice is futile speculation, practice without theory is incommunicable' (Roethlisberger, 1955); and theoretical sources may provide, in communicable form, concepts on which a frame of reference may be built, as a basis from which any organisation may begin to be analysed and understood.

The literature is extensive, and in this brief and introductory text nothing in the way of a comprehensive review is possible. Neither is it appropriate to present one categorical frame of reference: for theories of organisation and systems of administration based on them are in continuous process of evolution. A later chapter will provide some guidance for those who wish to read more widely, but in the meantime nothing more is being attempted than to present a variety of concepts in illustration of the thesis that there are 'ways of looking at' organisations, and at administrative processes, which can illuminate the nature of the task of administration, irrespective of the type of organisation in which it is being practised.

I. BUREAUCRACY

It is perhaps logical to begin with a concept which has acquired a pejorative connotation, and is commonly applied to a type of organisation which we do not like. Shorn of its emotional nimbus, the concept emerges as a measuring stick for some of the characteristics of any formal organisation. Whatever visions of red tape the word may evoke, sociologically a bureaucracy is to be defined unemotionally and straightforwardly as 'the type of organisation designed to accomplish large scale administrative tasks by systematically co-ordinating the work of many individuals' (Blau, 1963).

Max Weber (1864–1920), to whom we owe the concept, identified the main characteristics of a 'pure' bureaucracy. Although no live organisation corresponds exactly to his model, Weber's 'ideal type' provides a formula for analysing any large-scale organisation. Briefly, the major features of bureaucracy according to Weber (Gerth, 1948) are as follows:

1. A clear cut division of labour, with activities distributed in a fixed way as official duties.
2. A correlation between the distribution of duties and a formal administrative hierarchy, in which each office is supervised by the one above it.
3. A system of rules and regulations.
4. The exclusion of personal considerations from the conduct of official business.
5. Salaried employment based on technical qualifications, and constituting a career within the hierarchy.

Finally, 'bureaucratisation offers above all the optimum possibility for carrying through the principle of specialising administrative functions according to purely objective considerations.' In other words, according to Weber, it is administratively efficient.

If a quick mental review of any social work agency corroborates the existence, albeit in varying degrees, of these characteristics, then we have already learned something about the nature of the organisation with which the social work administrator has to deal. We also have a basis from which to assess some of the strengths and strains of its formal structure, and what lies behind both its smooth running and its tensions. Specialisation for example, may promote efficiency through the economical use of skills: but it may also limit the scope available for the imaginative deployment of those skills. Rules and regulations may promote a desirable impartiality of treatment; but they may also prevent the effective meeting of individual need, or serve to provide a shelter behind which the official may hide. (The regulations to which the National Assistance Board Officer must adhere, illustrate this bureaucratic dilemma.) Empha-

28

sis on the 'office' rather than the 'person' may promote stability, and even protect the life of the organisation: the 'office' of Children's Officer for example, has a legal identity quite irrespective of the person who holds it, and when a Children's Officer leaves, the Local Authority is legally required to fill the position. But there is no such protection in the case of the Leader of the less bureaucratic Family Service Unit. The formality of bureaucratic structure may be conducive to stability, but resistant to change; it may produce impartiality of treatment, both of employees and clients, but reduce individualisation.

This list of conflicts could be extended, but enough has perhaps been said to make the main point: against Weber's model, the administrator can begin to measure the characteristics of his own organisation, and to identify the elements in it which contribute to or detract from its effectiveness, and which require adjustment if it is to function as he thinks it should.

This said, however, it is to be recognised that Weber does not give the whole picture (see Gouldner, 1955). While indicating the way in which employees relate to each other within the formal hierarchy, he has nothing to say about their informal relationships, or about how they 'feel' about the organisation. Furthermore, while postulating the efficiency of a bureaucratic structure, he does not consider what ends, or whose ends, the organisation is intended to serve. These two aspects of the life of organisations – their informal structure and their goals – will be looked at next.

2. THE ORGANISATION AS A SOCIAL SYSTEM

Weber's emphasis on the formal and rational aspects of organisations has affinities with 'scientific management'. As we have seen, however, the Hawthorne investigations indicated the existence of an influential psychological component, additional to the formal structure. Philip Selznick (1964) presents an approach to a synthesis between the two.

A formal organisation, says Selznick, is 'a rationally ordered instrument for the achievement of stated goals': it is an economy, which can be manipulated to increase its efficiency. But within the formal structure operates a 'non-rational' element, which cannot ever be fully absorbed into the formal design. This non-rational element, although a source of friction, is as vital a component of the organisation as the formal structure itself, and it is insufficient to regard the organisation simply as an economy, for it is also a *social system*. In this social system, the individual does not function exclusively within the role assigned to him in the formal structure, for 'individuals have a propensity . . . to spill over the boundaries of their segmentary roles, and to participate as *wholes*'. In Weber's interpretation, functions are assigned to official positions, and not to individuals as such. In fact they are assigned to individual personalities 'who have interests and goals which do not always coincide with the goals of the formal system'. The individual brings to his work the needs of his own personality, a set of established habits, and possibly commitments to groups outside the organisation. As a result, he may resist demands made upon him in his official role. Effective control is unattainable without consent; and the organisation is therefore to be looked on as a co-operative system, with control depending on the active consent of participating individuals. Changes in the formal structure have effects which are not restricted to the 'formal organisation' alone, but impinge on its members as persons. An example may be drawn from the field of Child Care. The introduction of a Training Officer into a Children's Department, as far as formal structure is concerned, involves the incorporation of a new position into the hierarchy, and the clarification of formal lines of communication: all of which may be lucidly worked out on paper. It also affects existing social groupings within the agency; it may impinge on activities which individuals have come to regard as their own province; and it may dash the aspirations of any who hoped for promotion themselves. The incorporation of the new position into the formal structure is necessary for the co-ordination of activities; and the acceptance of the idea of change, and of the holder of the new position into the network of existing relationships, is essential if active consent is to be obtained.

We now see something of the potentially conflicting elements which go to make up an organisation. Firstly, not only does the formal structure itself have conflicting implications, in relation for example, to stability on the one hand and change on, the other, but in addition the organisation comprises informal relationships between people. Secondly, the members of an organisation do not react to situations exclusively in terms of their official positions, but also as whole persons, with feelings and aspirations of their own. Thirdly, the goals of individuals may not coincide with the stated goals of the organisation.

If these points hold good, the administrator will be concerned not only with the management of the 'formal' part of the organisation. He must also administer the social system.

But the one thing that all the members of this social system have in common is their employment within the organisation, for whose purposes they have been collected together. The nature of these purposes, and their implications for individuals, are directly relevant to the integration of the individual into the ongoing life of the organisation, and to any attempt to ensure that the formal structure and the informal social system are geared to compatible objectives.

3. ORGANISATIONAL GOALS

Weber stresses the rationality and efficiency of bureacratic structure, but efficiency can be assessed only in relation to desired ends; and once the goals of any organisation come to be analysed, they appear more complex than at first they seemed. 'Sometimes social workers talk as if the social services exist in order to provide a setting in which they can practise their casework skills' (Winnicott, 1964). But is the provision of a social work service the only objective of a Children's Department, or a Probation Department, or a Child Guidance Clinic? Organisation theory offers hypotheses about goals which are generic to all organisations – social work agencies included.

All organisations are predominantly oriented towards specific objectives, such as making a profit or giving a service. These goals serve a variety of functions (Etzioni, 1964). They justify the organisation's existence; provide a focus for its activities; and provide standards for assessing its efficiency. They may appear in written form, in legislation or a charter. An organisation may have more than one specific goal, as for example a University, which engages in both teaching and research, or a teaching hospital, which both treats patients and trains medical students. Where there are multiple goals, there is potential conflict. In a University, how is staff time to be allocated as between teaching and research, or money as between research equipment and classrooms?

And although organisations may be founded on specific goals, these may be modified, added to, or even replaced; for no organisation is static, and its 'real' goals evolve with it.

A clear example is the emergence of 'prevention' as a major objective of Children's Departments. Goals may be modified by a power group within the organisation, by a strong personality in a powerful position, or by pressures impinging from outside.

Furthermore, once in operation, an organisation acquires needs of its own, and the situation may be reached in which rules and regulations seem to serve the organisation itself, rather than the purposes for which it was established. For one of the needs of an organisation is to keep itself in being, and resources may be directed towards this after the original goals have lost their validity. In the field of voluntary action may be found examples of organisations which have modified or replaced their goals in relation to changes in society; and others which persist in maintaining themselves while their specific goals become increasingly out-dated.

As the organisation has its own needs, so have its individual members. They may join an organisation for a safe job, or for promotion, or for an opportunity to pursue their professional interests, or as a stepping stone to a better job elsewhere; and their commitment to the stated goals of the organisation is not automatically to be assumed (Argyris, 1964).

So it is to be seen that the goals of an organisation and its members are not easily to be defined. They may be simple or complex, compatible or conflicting, amenable to change or resistant to it, explicit or unstated; and they may be differently interpreted and supported by individual employees – or by committee members, or clients. A guide through this complexity is suggested by the concept of the *primary task* (Rice, 1963), the thesis being that every organisation has one predominating task to do, and that all its activities must be subordinated to this. To identify the primary task may be simpler in a commercial undertaking than in, for example, a Probation Department. The concept is nevertheless relevant; for a clear sense of objectives, and of priorities, is a *sine qua non* for the effective deployment of resources.

To sum up, theories about organisational goals can provide the administrator both with some understanding of the diverse processes by which these goals evolve, and with a unifying concept as a basis for rationalising them.

4. THE ORGANISATION AND ITS ENVIRONMENT

So far it has been stressed that an organisation has its own identity, as a formal structure, and as a social system. Yet it does not exist independently of the world outside it. Even the 'total institution', with 'its barrier to social intercourse with the outside . . . built right into the physical plant' (Goffman, 1961) is dependent on the outside world for toleration of its existence; and the process of 'aggiornamento' within the Roman Catholic church suggests that even an organisation serving a religion must take stock of its position in a secular context. Organisations are both created out of society and impinge on it. For example, certain types of organisation, such as mass-production car factories, are possibly only at a certain stage of industrial development, but may themselves influence further industrialisation.

Out of the highly complex relationship between organisations and their environment, five points may be selected as of particular significance for administration, although in practice each of them interlocks with the others.

(i) An organisation derives its *sanctions* from society. What it must do, may do, or may not do, is in varying ways and degrees determined not within the organisation

34

itself, but by outside agents. Thus, the power and duties of a Local Authority department derive largely from Parliament, and on its performance of these depends a significant part of its income. A voluntary agency may, though within limits, define its own spheres of activity; but it depends on the community for the financial resources to translate policy into practice. An important element in policy development for any organisation will be 'determining the relationship of the organisation to the larger society, which in turn becomes a question of what the society (or elements within it) wants done, or can be persuaded to support'. (Thompson, 1964)

(ii) The very *structure* of organisations is affected by the social environment. In an industrialised society, the small family business yields ground to the larger factory; rapidly expanding areas demand the development of structures for the administration of local government; and large scale organisation accompanied by specialisation tends to become characteristic. 'All organisations consist of a concept and a *structure.* . . . The structure holds the concept, and furnishes the instrumentalities for bringing it into the world of facts and action. . . .' (Sumner, 1906) New concepts, such as a National Health Service, or the removal of young people from the jurisdiction of the courts, require for their implementation both sanctions and a structure: and the new structure can be devised only in relation to structures which already exist.

(iii) Organisations are affected by *technological developments* within their social environment. Automation affects the number of people employed in relation to output, expenditure on equipment as compared with salaries, the type of skills which must be recruited; and indeed every aspect of both the formal and the informal structure of an organisation. Advances in psychiatric medicine not only affect the

35

treatment of individual patients, but demand the restructuring of the mental hospital from a 'care' to a 'treatment' organisation. In the social services, the development of professional knowledge and skills in social work alters the relationship between the lay administrator and his social work staff; and it may affect the objectives which the agency sets for itself, its methods of working, and the numbers and nature of its establishment. A sensitive response to relevant technology is a condition of an organisation's efficiency in a changing society.

(iv) Organisations reflect the *value systems* of their social environment. For example, some writers have postulated an affinity between protestantism and the 'private enterprise' pattern of industrial organisations (Weber, 1958, and Tawney, 1926); whereas a nationalised industry is an expression of a different philosophy of the ownership of wealth. An American social worker has suggested that 'the British social services result from a philosophy about the relationship of the State to the citizen, which has been translated into declared national policy' (Osborn, 1958). This monocausal explanation oversimplifies, but some justification for it is to be found in any piece of social legislation. The Children and Young Persons Act (1933) made specific the circumstances under which society considered that children and young persons 'ought' to be brought before a court, and the Children Act (1948) aims at a balance between the rights of parents and the needs of children. All organisations catering for criminal offenders are caught up in the punishment/treatment dilemma, which they cannot resolve internally, because the sanctions under which they operate represent a compromise on the part of society. The physical structure of new prisons, within which the prison as an organisation has to function, exemplifies the problem in tangible form.

(v) Yet another element in an organisation's environment are the *other organisations with which it interacts.* Some of this interaction may be specifically regulated, for example by legislation which sets limits to an organisation's scope; or by formal agreements, as between Trade Unions and Employers' Federations; or by a 'superior' organisation, such as the Home Office in respect of certain activities of Children's and Probation Departments. In so far as interaction between any one organisation and others is not formally regulated, there is scope for the processes of conflict or co-operation; and a need for a clear identification of the points at which interaction is of importance. Statutory social services for children at local level provide an example of a mixture of regulated and informal interaction – their duties and limits regulated by legislation and by their position within the formal structure of Local Authority or Petty Sessional Division, but their effectiveness extensively dependent also on their informal interaction with each other.

5. CHANGE

A characteristic common to all the attributes of organisations so far discussed – formal structure, social system, goals, and environment – is that they are subject to change, and Professor Titmuss' (1958) description of a social service as 'a dynamic process and not a finished article' applies equally appropriately to any organisation. Even to maintain itself in existence, an organisation must in some degree adjust to its changing environment. One of the characteristics traditionally attributed to bureaucracy is resistance to change, but recently it has been suggested that 'the only permanence in bureaucratic structures is the occurrence of change in predictable patterns, and even these are not unalterably fixed' (Blau, 1963). Change is not to be escaped, and the response of administrators to this fact can mean stagnation or vitality for an organisation.

Sociologists have traditionally focussed primarily on the 'orderly' characteristics of social systems, rather than on the systematic analysis of the factors which further change (Moore, 1963). Lippitt and his colleagues, however, explore one aspect of change which is of particular significance for the formulation and implementation of policy: change which is *planned*. 'All dynamic systems', they say, 'reveal a continuous process of change – adaptation, adjustment, re-organisation. That is what we mean by being dynamic, by being alive' (Lippitt, 1958). But change comes about in a variety of ways. As an organisation is confronted by new internal or external situations, it is challenged to change its structure or its ways of functioning – as a Local Authority Welfare Department may be by an intake, for the first time, of trained social workers; or a voluntary organisation by new social legislation. In this kind of situation, an organisation may mobilise its own resources in a deliberate response to the challenge, or it may passively allow change to 'evolve'. Here are two very different ways of responding, both to developmental changes within the organisation, and to changes impinging on it from outside.

There is a further distinction to be made: between external change facing an organisation, and to which its response may be active or passive, and *planned* change originating from within, either as a response to a specific problem, or on the discovery that improvement is possible (Lippitt, 1958).

Training in methods of promoting planned change has probably been most fully developed in the fields of psychiatry, clinical psychology, and social work, rather than in relation to organisations (Lippitt, 1958); but there may be a useful analogy between the caseworker's role as a 'change agent' *vis-à-vis* the client, and the administrator's role in the agency.

6. WORK AND RESOURCES

A further concept, developed in particular by the Glacier Institute of Management, is that all organisations have work to do, and resources with which to do it. To achieve its objectives, an organisation does work of a kind impossible to isolated individuals; and this work requires resources of a kind which individuals alone cannot provide. (A corollary of this is that the individual social worker is as dependent on his agency for the resources he needs to do his professional work, as it is on him.) The resources of an organisation are human (e.g. skills), material (e.g. accommodation and equipment), and time (e.g. the man hours available for the completion of work); and money as a resource is basic to all of these.

Within the organisation, each individual member himself does work, and commands resources. The Probation Officer for example cannot function without drawing on the resources of the Probation Department, but he himself has some degree of control over the deployment of his personal professional skills, and those of his typist, and over the use of his time.

The concept of an organisation as consisting of work and resources is one which can provide a particularly useful starting point for administration, which could be described as the *process of organising resources to get work done*. In this definition, anyone who controls some of the resources of an organisation, and deploys them in relation to work, is an administrator. To this extent, even the social worker, in so far as he deploys time and skill in the agency's service, is performing a task which includes an administrative component.

7. TYPES OF FORMAL ORGANISATION

Organisations have so far been presented as having generic characteristics, and illustrations have been drawn from factories, mental hospitals, prisons, social work agencies, and the Roman Catholic church. Strung together thus, such a list gives an immediate impression of diversity. Having considered the characteristics which organisations share, it is realistic to explore the features which make one 'kind' of organisation different from another; including those which are characteristic of social work agencies. Even here there is diversity, for a Family Service Unit obviously differs from a Probation Department. Yet even in looking at diversity, it will be necessary to bear in mind the generic characteristics already considered, for they too are part of the nature of all social work agencies.

An extensive range of characteristics is available as a basis for differentiation — or comparison. One might select such factors as size, type of ownership, source of income, sanctions, or the specific purposes served; by all of which the task of administration will be affected. Theorists have searched for a basis of classification, and the following references may serve to illustrate the potential relevance of their thinking to the administration of social work agencies.

(i) A distinction may be made between 'production' organisations, whose technical personnel work with things, and 'service' organisations where they work with people (Blau, 1963). The criteria of efficiency will obviously differ in the two types, and if a service organisation is to 'put itself across', it will have to find a different way of doing so from the factory's production figures. It may also be that in social work agencies the 'service' element can be seen to have particular relevance for administration; for the administrator, no less than the social worker, works with people rather than things.

Furthermore, organisations may be classified according to the category of persons *for whose benefit* they operate (Blau, 1963). The 'prime beneficiary' of the mutual benefit association (e.g. a Friendly Society) is the membership; that of the business concern, the owners; that of the 'commonweal' organisation (e.g. the Police Force) the public-at-large; and that of the service organisation, the client. The basic function of the service organisation is to serve its clients: and within this category may be placed hospitals, schools, and social work agencies. The important problems of such organisations seem to centre around the provision of professional services: around the administration of such services to those who seek them out, need them, or are required to accept them. Of these problems, perhaps the most crucial is the potential conflict between the professional culture of those members of staff through whom the service reaches the client, and the bureaucratic structure and culture of the agency as a formal organisation.

(ii) Another distinguishing feature of different types of organisation is their system of *values* (Parsons, 1960), which defines their basic orientation to their work. The value system of a business firm is linked to production, and success is measured in terms of profit. What constitutes the value system of a social work agency? And how does such an agency measure its success? The formulation of objectives, the methods by which they are pursued, and the criteria of progress all depend on precision in relation to questions such as these.

(iii) A further basis of comparison (Etzioni, 1961) may be

the *type of authority* with which the members of an organisation are willing to, or must, comply: the coercive authority of an army or a prison, for example, compared with the normative or value-based authority of a religious or professional organisation. The concept of authority will be explored later, the point here being that the type of authority appropriate to one type of organisation is not necessarily appropriate to another; as the army major may discover when on discharge he becomes a Personnel Manager in a factory. For social work agencies, a major question is whether such agencies have characteristics which make it appropriate for administrators to exercise authority by certain means rather than by others, if authority is to be willingly accepted.

To conclude, the points raised in this chapter are intended to illustrate the contribution which theory can make to explaining the nature of organisations, which are the context within which administration is practised. With this as background, the nature of administration itself may now be considered.

III

The nature of administration

I. ADMINISTRATION AS A METHOD

Administration takes places in organisations – in social units formed for specific purposes. The organisation, with its formal structure, social groupings, environment, resources, and goals, is the material with which the administrator works, as the social worker works with the personality and situation of the client. The administrator's job, like that of the social worker, is to get something done, through the process of organising resources in relation to objectives. The Child Care Officer or Probation Officer organising home visits on a time-saving basis is performing a task with an administrative element; as is the Medical Social Worker deciding what categories of patients might most usefully be referred to her on admission to hospital. Each is consciously attempting to use time and professional skills as efficiently as may be in relation to the agency's 'service' function.

The social worker is involved in administration in two major ways. He himself controls resources and is responsible for organising them; and since the agency is an organic unit, and he a part of it, his own activities cannot be self-contained. There is an interdependence of organisation and individual which cannot be escaped. As the social worker, or the clerk, moves up in the formal hierarchy, the 'organising' element in his role increases, and with it the share of the agency's resources over which he has control. Within the formal structure, a major difference between Probation Officer and Principal Probation Officer, or between Child Care Officer and Children's Officer lies in the extent of their control over resources, and of their authority for deploying them. This is a difference of degree rather than of kind. A difference in kind may be seen in respect of function: the 'specialist' function of the social worker in a role utilising social work skill, as distinct from the 'executive' function of the administrator, whose primary task is the maintenance of the organisation, or his particular section of it, as an ongoing concern.

The relationship between the specialist and the administrator is affected by the understanding which each has of the other's function. The administrator needs to recognise that the specialist, by virtue of his training and experience, is an expert within his own area of competence; while the specialist must understand that the administrator's function relates directly to the organisation as a whole. One might use as an example questions related to taking a child into care. The Child Care Officer as a specialist is the member of staff competent to formulate and present the case of a particular child. The Children's Officer, however, must weigh in the balance factors which are outside the individual Child Care Officer's range of competence — such as the pressure on places in Foster Homes or Residential Homes, or the application of a uniform policy throughout the whole of the Department. In this illustration, administration appears both as an activity of a distinct kind (for the factors taken into consideration by the Children's Officer differ from those considered by the Child Care

Officer), and as a process by which the specialist's functions are affected (for the Child Care Officer may need to accept a final decision made not by himself, but by the Children's Officer).

A difficulty of the social worker in such situations may be a reluctance to accept that the 'professional' part of his activities cannot be kept separate from the administrative procedures of the agency. A further example might be the completion by a Child Care Officer of the forms which record the transfer of a child from a Children's Home to a foster mother. This is an administrative process in that it co-ordinates activities within the agency – the movement of the child with the payment of the foster mother; but it also forms a part of the social worker's professional responsibility to take the necessary steps to ensure that the foster mother is promptly paid.

For the social worker promoted to a senior administrative position, a difficulty may be that, while welcoming the promotion, he may nevertheless be reluctant to relinquish his social work (i.e. his specialist) role, in favour of the executive one which the new position demands. Thus, he may both fail to be effective as an administrator, and at the same time tend to usurp some of the area of discretion which properly belongs to the social worker now below him in the hierarchy.

Enough has perhaps been said to indicate that although certain individuals within an agency carry roles which are specifically administrative–i.e. concerned with organisation – nevertheless every member of the agency is *ipso facto* a member of the administrative team, and works in an administrative setting. Some knowledge of what administration is about, and some willingness and ability to participate in it, are directly relevant to the social worker's role as an employee.

Later chapters will be concerned with analysing the position, functions, and tasks of the administrator as such. What an administrator does, however, and how he does it, will obviously in some measure be determined by his own conception of administration. We have considered already some 'ways of looking at' organisations, and may now as a preliminary to a more specific approach, submit administration to a similar process, thus both suggesting frames of reference for administrators, and indicating the potential contribution of dynamic administration to any organisation.

It will be well to begin with some working definitions, to serve us from now on:

(i) *Administration* is the process by which the total activities of an organisation are directed towards its objectives. It is thus a *purposive* process.

(ii) An *administrator* is a member of the organisation who has authority for directing and co-ordinating the work of subordinates. (Thus in a social work agency a social worker is not an administrator, and neither is a clerk; an Area Child Care Officer or a Chief Clerk is.)

(iii) The *executive system* is the hierarchy of positions from which the organisation is administered. (This can be clearly seen in a highly structured organisation such as a unit of the Civil Service, where the area of authority of each rank is very specifically defined. It may not always be so easily distinguished in social work agencies which are less 'bureaucratised'.)

(iv) The *Executive* is the holder of the position at the top of the formal hierarchy: the Principal Probation Officer or the Family Service Unit Leader, for example. This is the position in which overall administrative authority is vested, and from which the widest range of administrative activity flows.

(v) In respect of social work services, the *'organisation'* may be taken to be the social work agency itself: an identifiable unit over which one Executive exercises authority. Thus in a hospital, the Medical Social Work Department is the Senior Social Worker's unit of organisation; and the hospital is part of its environment.

Of all the attributes so far suggested as characteristic of organisations, one at least is indisputable: organisations are composed of people. The study of administrative methods has been defined as 'the study of people at work, their behaviour, their relationships, the way work is split up between different roles' (Brown, 1960). Whatever tools the administrator uses – and regulations and form-filling may be amongst them – the two major components of his raw material are people and work. Even for money he is dependent on the people who control it; and even if he acts as if staff were chessmen to be moved at will, his insensitivity will not eliminate the 'human element'. People will still have feelings about him, and about their work, which will affect the way in which they function. The criterion for any administrative procedures, in any organisation, is whether they enable the organisation, as a group of people working together with a shared purpose, to do a better job. Administration is thus primarily a problem-solving and enabling process; it involves the making of decisions; and, if only because present decisions affect future functioning, it is directed towards the future.

2. FOUR CENTRAL CONCEPTS

Leadership and decision-making, authority and communication, are four approaches to the organisation of people and work which may serve as an orientation for the later discussion of the specific functions of administrators.

(a) Leadership

Leadership has been described as 'a slippery phenomenon, the precise nature of which eludes both common sense and social science' (Selznick, 1957). There may be some indiv- iduals who are more likely than others to become leaders, but whether or not this is so, leadership is a particular kind of activity, the nature of which is determined by the social situations which leaders are called upon to handle. The task of the 'interpersonal' leader is to evoke personal devotion, and to smooth the path of personal relationships: 'he is more concerned with persons than with policies.' The *in- stitutional* leader has different tasks to perform. Thus in Selznick's view, the function of the Executive as institu- tional leader, (which does not exclude him from 'inter- personal' leadership as well), is 'to transform a neutral body of people into a working group committed to the value premises of the organisation's policy'. Responding to such leadership, *everybody* in a social work agency, and not just the social workers, would be committed to the agency's objectives. The following tasks are demanded of the institutional leader:

1. The creative and continuous setting of objectives, for 'once an organisation becomes a "going concern" it can readily escape the task of defining its purpose.'
2. Not only the making of policy, but its implementation, through building it into the structure of the organisa- tion.
3. To protect and promote the values for which the organisation stands.
4. To promote co-operation between internal interest groups.

Barnard suggests that successful leadership requires that the leader be personally committed to the declared purposes of the organisation. This commitment on his part is the 'inescapable element in creating a desire for adherence ... on the part of those whose efforts, willingly contributed, constitute organisation' (Barnard, 1938). Selznick and Barnard alike see the value element in leadership as central: and this is indeed a 'personal' attribute. But Selznick's four 'tasks' suggest specific ways in which leadership can find practical expression through the formal exercise of executive responsibility.

A typology of institutional leadership is provided by Johns (1963) who suggests that it may be broadly of two kinds: it may be directed essentially at maintaining the organisation, or it may be focussed on change. The first type is characterised by efforts to keep the organisation 'going in its established ways', and in so far as an organisation needs continuity, it is essential. But if as suggested in the last chapter, one characteristic of an organisation and its environment is continuous change, then leadership for planned change is no less relevant.

The Executive's position of authority does not make him a leader; but leadership may be an essential aspect of his role, to be assumed not exclusively by virtue of his personal qualities, but also through the performance of quite specific activities.

(b) Decision-making

The actual job of carrying out an agency's function is done by the social workers. In the case of the Probation Service, for example, the Morison Committee went so far as to suggest that a Principal Probation Officer should carry a caseload 'only if it is clear that his duties as a Principal will not suffer' (Home Office, 1962). What then is the part played in the accomplishment of the agency's task by the

Executive, whose direct and on-going contact with clients may be minimal? One role has already been suggested: that of providing leadership, in the formulation and implementation of policy. This involves making decisions – choosing particular courses of action, and rejecting others. Although it is the social worker who works with the client, it is at Executive level that decisions are made which may determine the size and nature of his caseload, and thus to some degree at least the quality of service he can give. The Executive affects the work of an agency because the decisions which he has the authority to make, influence the performance of the specialists through whom the service reaches the client. For example, the way he deploys resources and assigns specific tasks, helps to determine what the social worker is free to do. The task of the Executive is to set up an administrative organisation in which the decisions open to the specialists – the social workers – are influenced consistently towards the more effective performance of the agency's tasks. Decisions, at any level, are 'correct' if they select the 'means appropriate to reach designated ends' (Simon, 1961). Effective decision-making thus presupposes the greatest possible clarity about what the organisation's objectives are.

A topical example of an important 'decision-making area' is the establishment of 'preventive services' within Children's Departments. The decision is made to appoint Family Caseworkers, as distinct from Child Care Officers, and subsequent decisions relate to the way in which they are to be fitted into the existing structure, and as to how cases are to be allocated to them. But what is the primary task of a Children's Department? Is it to prevent children from coming into care? Or to provide for them while they are in care? Are these two tasks to be kept separate from each other? And are the social work functions and methods of a Family Caseworker so different from those of a Child Care Officer as to require that the two be kept separate in the formal agency structure? These seem to be the sort of questions about which it is relevant to reach decisions *before* the process of incorporating new social workers into the agency is begun. Unless this is done, it is likely that a situation will crystallise in which a 'Family Casework' section will be found to have acquired a separate identity, function, and structure, almost by default. The need is for the Executive to make decisions 'with one eye on the matter before him, and one eye on the effect of *this* decision upon the future pattern: that is upon its organisational consequences' (Simon, 1961). For decisions made now help to determine what decisions will be possible in the future.

Part of an Executive's decision-making function is to distinguish between matters which can safely be left as they are, and those on which it is important that decisions should be consciously and deliberately made. The methods by which he identifies issues which demand action, reaches decisions upon them, and implements them, form the very core of the administrative process.

Whether the role of the Executive is interpreted in terms of leadership or of decision-making, two concepts, authority and communication, appear so integral to it that they demand special consideration.

(c) Authority

In casework, the concept of authority is familiar to the professional social worker, who must come to terms with its psychological significance for both himself and his client, accept it as an unavoidable component in the relationship between them, and find a basis for reconciling the authority vested in the social worker with the client's right of self-determination.

If authority is inherent in the relationship between social worker and client, it is no less a component of the interaction between superiors and subordinates in the administration of organisations. How do social workers react to the suggestion that they fill subordinate positions? And yet their position within the executive system of their employing organisations is a reality; and so is the authority vested in those of higher rank, whether they be trained social workers or not. Practising social workers find that their professional authority does not extend to cover the full range of their activities: in some matters they have to accept the authority of others. And social workers promoted to administrative positions find that authority is now an element in their relationship with subordinates, both professional and lay, instead of with clients. Furthermore, it relates to matters which are administrative in character, rather than exclusively professional; and it has to be exercised in relation to those with whom the administrator may for a long time have worked as a professional colleague.

Authority is as relevant a concept for the administrator as it is for the social worker; with the additional complexity that it concerns not only the relationship between one individual and another, but the positions and functions of both of them within the organisation.

Authority may be defined as *the power to make decisions which determine the conduct of others*. Not all the behaviour of subordinates is determined by the authority of superiors: but the superior exercises authority when, if he makes a decision or gives an order, it is accepted. Power over others may be bestowed by *position*; as is extensively the case in an army, where an officer is obeyed, i.e. successfully exercises authority, because of his rank. Another type of authority is *legal,* with obedience owed not to a position, or to a person, but to enacted rules. Yet another type is the *professional* or technical authority accorded to an expert by virtue of his special knowledge or skill. And finally there is the authority described by Weber as *'charismatic',* resting on the personal devotion of follower to leader. This is the only kind of authority which is truly 'personal'; a point worth remembering as a counterbalance to any tendency to regard the personality of the administrator as the only factor determining his behaviour. Each of these types of authority is relevant to the administration of social work agencies. Authority accrues to the Children's Officer by virtue of his *position* at the point of interaction between the Children's Department and the Children's Committee; Children's Officer and Child Care Officers alike are subject to the *legal* authority of legislation and Statutory Rules and Regulations; the Training Officer or Casework Supervisor will expect to carry *professional* authority as an expert on social work practice; and the qualities of the Children's Officer as a leader will determine the *charismatic* authority accorded to him personally.

Of all these types of authority, two seem to call for particular attention. For in practice one of the most difficult tasks of the Executive may be the clarification of the boundaries between the authority vested in his own *position,* and the *professional* authority of his social work staff.

One function of authority is to secure co-ordination, so that one plan – for example a duty rota – will control the activities of all involved. A traditional mechanism is 'unity of command', each individual accepting the authority of one person only: one man, one boss. This pattern distributes authority to particular executive positions, and places the administrator in authority over the specialist. Besides being simpler on paper than in practice, it has two major draw-backs. The specialist is likely to resist the authority of the administrator in matters in which he considers himself to be the more competent; and if the specialist is to be used to the full, decisions requiring his particular knowledge and skill must be left to him.

Authority exercised by administrators is essential, for without it the activities of the organisation cannot be co-ordinated. On the other hand, the specialist claims authority within the sphere of his professional competence. The clash is a fundamental one, which perhaps can never be fully resolved. (An example is the opposition of G.P.'s to the extension of administrative authority which they consider salaried employment would imply.)

But a solution may at least be sought in the division of authority according to subject matter. The administrator may retain his 'organising' authority but, regarding the specialist not simply as a subordinate, but as holding a position partly *outside* the executive system, accord him the fullest possible autonomy in professional matters.

Where roles are fully professionalised, the specialist him-self is in a position to assume such authority: no one ques-tions the professional autonomy of the surgeon. In social work agencies the position is less clear, for not all those who hold social work (i.e. specialist) positions embody the commonly recognised attributes of a profession. Further-more, the distribution of positions as between laymen and professionals in social work agencies is extremely varied. No full discussion of it can be attempted here (see Etzioni, 1964), but two examples may be given of the importance of a clear demarcation of administrative as distinct from pro-fessional authority. Local Authority Welfare Departments with lay administrators are recruiting trained social workers. Is the authority relationship to remain a purely hierarchical one : or is the lay administrator to recognise that the knowledge and skills of the newcomers are credentials for a degree of authority not previously accorded to those at field work level? Secondly, Children's Departments are introducing Casework Supervisors. What are the limits of authority of a casework supervisor in relation to a Senior Child Care Officer, whose authority over Child Care Officers has previously been professional as well as administrative?

In conclusion of this brief introduction to a complex question, four general points are suggested for consideration. Firstly, the only valid reason for using authority is to get the job done. This may provide an acceptable rationale for those to whom the exercise of authority in respect of former colleagues comes hard. Mary Follett (Metcalf, 1941) suggests a basis for 'depersonalising' it: discover and make clear what the *situation* (and not the person in authority) demands, and unite all concerned in obeying that. Secondly, the authority delegated to any individual, executive or specialist, must be commensurate with the job to be done. He must be given the authority to make the decisions and use the resources which the effective performance of the job demands. Thirdly, while authority in terms of power to make decisions and use resources can be delegated, responsibility can only be assumed. The social worker may be given the authority needed to do his work, for which he certainly *feels* responsible. But the fact that every member of any agency feels responsible for his job, and is accountable to his senior for the performance of it, does not divest the Executive of any element of his 'organisational' responsibility for the agency as a whole. Fourthly, although it is integral to the administrator's role, authority is not the only basis of the relationship between superior and subordinate in the executive system: influence and persuasion are no less important.

(d) Communication

The 'scientific managers' saw the formal hierarchy of authority as a channel of communication from top to bottom, primarily for the transmission of orders. Subsequently, communication upwards was recognised as serving the purpose of providing the executive system with the information needed for making decisions. For example, it is only from the social workers that the Executive of an agency can keep himself informed about the needs of clients, and about difficulties in the implementation of policy. Using this source of information efficiently, he may well 'keep in touch' more effectively than by carrying a caseload himself.

A formal channel of communication is an essential element in organisation, all too often left unclear. The *formal* communications system, deliberately constructed, is the 'official hierarchy'; and communication through it is a two way process. Decisions and information are transmitted downwards, and information flows upwards. Barnard (1938) identifies the characteristics of an efficient formal system. The channel should be clearly known; reach every member of the organisation; be as short as possible; and the whole of it should normally be used (a communication up or down should not by-pass any executive position). These are matters of direct practical relevance, when for example an agency is in process of decentralising, and thus of reconstructing its executive system.

In practice, however, communication channels cannot be correlated exclusively with channels of authority. Communication flows not only upwards and downwards but laterally; and the formal system is supplemented by an informal communication network, based on the social interaction of individuals. Through this network flows information, advice, 'shop', gossip; and it may produce a situation in which individuals accept leadership from outside the executive system. One possibility is the formation of 'cliques' of individuals seeking to meet their own needs; while alternatively friendliness and co-operation within the informal system may promote efficiency rather than hinder it.

A source of tension in any organisation is the incompatibility of its formal and informal aspects – its formal structure and its social system. It thus becomes the task of the executive not only to construct the essential formal channel of communication, but to promote the kind of personal relationships, and attitudes of goodwill towards the organisation, which may produce an informal communication network congruous with the formal system rather than at odds with it.

Whatever specific purposes communication serves in the transmission of information or the implementation of decisions, it can also serve to strengthen the bonds between individual and organisation. The organisation achieves its purposes through the behaviour of all its members. Yet each individual joins an organisation for his own purposes; and what he wants from it, and what it needs from him, can be reconciled only if the purposes of the organisation are made clear, and if the individual finds an acceptable role for himself in relation to them. Unless the Housemother understands and accepts the rehabilitative function of the Children's Department, there will be confusion over the uses of a Children's Home, and frustration for the Housemother. Unless the reception clerk understands the spirit as well as the letter of an agency's function, those in need of service may not get it. And unless executive and social work staff share a common purpose, the agency will lack a sense of direction. But purpose can be shared only if understood, and implemented only if each individual both understands and accepts the role expected of him. Communication is a basic tool in the clarification of shared purpose, and the involvement of individuals in it.

As has been seen, communication ramifies throughout an organisation: but the primary responsibility for using it effectively to translate policy into action rests with administrators; and particularly with the Executive. To keep the channels clear, and to decide what to communicate, and when, and how, and to whom, is a major administrative task.

On the technical aspects of ensuring that people understand what other people mean this brief comment on communication has not touched (see Simon, 1961). Two examples of failure to communicate may, however, provide 'thinking points':

(i) The Director of a Local Authority Welfare Department holds monthly staff meetings, at which social workers pass on information, and are invited to express opinions. One of them says 'it doesn't help very much, because nothing ever seems to come of it, and we don't really know what the meetings are for'.

(ii) A Children's Officer says that his Child Care Officers do not understand the limits to his authority, or the pressures under which he must work. He never tells them.

In conclusion of this presentation of the nature of administration, the following points may be recapitulated:

(i) Administration is the process of organising resources to get work done.

(ii) Although certain roles are specifically administrative, every member of an organisation, specialists included, is part of the administrative structure.

(iii) The setting of administration is the organisation: through it must the administrator work.

(iv) Leadership, decision-making, authority, and communication are essential ingredients of the administrative process.

PART TWO

Social work administration

IV

The special nature of social work agencies

Although the emphasis so far has been on generic aspects of organisations and of administration, the illustrations from social work agencies could equally well have come from the civil service or industry. The Executive of a social work agency heads an organisation of which the components are a formal structure; groups and individuals interacting with each other; objectives, whether explicit or not; an environment to which the agency is organically linked; and resources with which work is to be done. Furthermore change, planned or unplanned, is inherent in any organisation. These six characteristics are suggested as a basic frame of reference for social work administrators seeking to understand the nature of their own working environment, and to find a useful role within it.

Administration too has generic aspects: it is everywhere concerned with determining objectives and formulating policy; with acquiring and allocating resources; and with maintaining and evaluating performance. In other words, it has to *direct* the organisation; to *manage* it; and to *supervise* its day-to-day activities. Leadership, decision-making, the exercise of authority, and the establishment and maintenance of an effective communication system are relevant to factory and social work administration alike.

We have also seen that organisations can be classified according to type. Social work administration must respond to the special attributes of *social work agencies as such*, which thus need to be recognised as clearly as possible. Using the ideas suggested in Chapter II as a basis for classifying organisations, we may now consider some features generic to social work agencies, and of particular significance for social work administration. For useful though ideas drawn from industrial management may be, it is not to be assumed that they can be applied to social work agencies without some adaptation: for these are organisations of a very different type.

I. CHARACTERISTICS COMMON TO SOCIAL WORK AGENCIES

(a) Service to clients

A social work agency is a *service* organisation, of which the primary task is to produce services, not goods. This has major implications.

Firstly, all organisations use both human and material resources, but the balance between them differs: goods are produced by machines, and services by people. Administration in a factory is concerned extensively with the efficient use of plant. In a social work agency, the major resource is human: the specialist personnel through whom the service which it is the agency's primary task to produce, reaches the client. The basic function of the social work administrator, be he agency head or in the middle range of administration, is to ensure that the social workers, the agency's 'means of production', are enabled to do a better job. The social worker promoted to an administrative position may no longer provide the service himself; but it is his function to enable others to do so. In a social work agency, a major aspect of the administrator's role is to work through staff, to ensure effective service for clients.

Secondly, whereas social workers work with clients, the agency as a whole exists to translate policy into practice, and to contribute to the resolution of social problems. If on a day-to-day basis it focuses on its existing clients, in the long run it must be concerned with helping to meet the needs, and utilising the resources, of the community in which it is located. This aspect of the social work administrator's function is clear in the case of the Organising Secretary of a Council of Social Service; but other examples to illustrate it could be planning for the use of voluntary helpers by the Probation and Aftercare Service; the identification of special problems of immigrant children and the mobilising of community resources to tackle them; membership of a Co-ordinating Committee; the working relationship between any Executive and the members of his Committee; or formal consultation on policy with the heads of other agencies.

Thirdly, because the major resources of social work agencies are human rather than material, there are particular difficulties in setting standards, and in evaluating performance, both of individuals and of the agency as a whole. Annual Reports typically describe what has been done during the year; but by what criteria is this to be evaluated? A social work agency cannot measure its output as can a factory, and yet if public money is to be well spent, and accountability to have real meaning, then objective criteria of efficiency need to be evolved. The introduction of Training Officers and of Staff Supervision, although primarily due to the need to provide support and assistance to untrained workers, may emerge as a useful method of setting, maintaining, and improving standards of social work service.

Fourthly, because the 'specialist' element is important, and because both the agency's major resources and the recipients of service are people, there is in social work agencies particular likelihood of conflict between the formal or 'bureaucratic' aspects of the agency, and the 'professional' ones. Probation Officers completing official forms may think that the time could be more profitably spent on interviewing; a Child Care Officer may have to make statutory visits which seem inappropriate to the needs of the casework situation; any social worker may feel that the policy of the agency conflicts with the needs of an individual client. The characteristics of a bureaucracy have both positive and negative aspects. On balance, it seems that the strengths of a bureaucracy lie in areas where uniformity and impersonality are important, and the weaknesses where individuality and the 'human element' need freer rein. The social work administrator must walk the tight-rope between the situation of the *agency as a whole*, which includes its formal system, and the external sanctions under which it operates; and the needs of the social work *specialist* in the service of individual clients. By and large, the tendency (and indeed the function) of the Executive will be to see the agency as a whole, and that of the social worker to focus on the needs of his own clients. Senior Officers – 'middle management' – almost invariably have to take the strain involved in standing between the two.

(b) Social work values

In their service to clients, social work agencies give expression to a *system of values* integral to social work training: respect for individual worth; for the right of the individual

64

to make his own decisions; for the individual's capacity for growth; for the right to the opportunity for growth, and so on. If such values have any validity at all, they are relevant not exclusively to clients, but to all human beings, members of staff included. Their incorporation by the social work administrator into his own working method is essential if tension between the 'specialist' and 'executive' aspects of the agency's life is to be minimised. It is also logical that in its internal affairs an agency should adhere to the values it professes in its work with clients.

For the social work administrator, the implications can be quite specific. For example:

(i) He must believe in the agency's purposes, and in social work as a method of serving them. The administrator is not a neutral agent, but a decision maker; and decision-making involves the use of value judgments, in the selection of choices between alternatives. His decisions need to be such as will make for a better social work service, and he must serve the organisation not for its own sake, but as a means to an end. Furthermore, *commitment* has already been suggested as one of the essential ingredients of leadership. The ideal Executive is one with whom all can identify, and the Executive who is uncommitted to social work values cannot offer leadership to a social work agency.

(ii) As social work values respect the client's needs and potentialities, so the administrator also must concern himself with the creative use of human resources. This will involve recognising the importance to staff members of due recognition and status; respecting the professional or technical competence of the individual, be he social worker or shorthand typist; and recognising the capacity and will of the individual to grow, with all that this demands in the way of professional supervision and opportunities for further training, special opportunity for the use of special skills, and appropriate prospects of promotion: in other words, 'staff development'.

(iii) The values of social work are essentially democratic. To conform, administrative methods need to be democratic too. A complex decision has been described as 'like a great river' (Simon, 1961) all the tributaries of which it may be impossible to trace; but one of the attributes of democratic administration will be the fullest possible involvement of all concerned in the processes by which decisions affecting them are reached.

The conflict between bureaucratic structure and professional culture is a real one; but it is part of the administrator's function to attempt to minimise it. And between the principles of 'good administration' and the values of social work, no basic conflict is to be found.

(c) Democratic authority

The question of democratic processes in agency administration leads logically to the third characteristic by which organisations may be 'typed': the type of *authority* with which their members are prepared willingly to comply.

In a social work agency, staff accept the authority of an administrator because of the power associated with his position; or the strength of legal sanctions; or because they respect him as a person. Additionally, because the agency relies on specialist personnel to do its work, the authority associated with professional knowledge and skill assumes particular significance.

In a highly bureaucratic system, the sources of authority are predominantly positional or legal, and find expression through the formal hierarchy. For example, the nurse accepts the authority of the Sister because of the formal position in which each stands in relation to the other. The social worker, however, does not fit easily into such a scheme of things as is literally illustrated by a Mental Hospital, recently reorganising, which did not know where to place the Psychiatric Social Worker on its new organisation chart.

First, as a specialist, the social worker stands partly outside the formal chain of command, exercising his own professional authority in his work with clients. (The reconciliation of legal and professional authority is approached in the Probation Order, where the document itself accords authority to the individual Probation Officer. Even here, however, it is the 'office' of the Probation Officer rather than his professional expertise that the Bench is formally recognising.)

Secondly, the professional social worker is likely to wish to accord priority to the authority of his own professional standards and values, acquired in the course of training. In a field of social work where professional training is now universal – medical social work – the Executive and the social workers are likely to share professional allegiances; the agency head is also normally the 'head social worker'; and departments are in any case small enough not to be bureaucratised. The situation is very different in the case of a statutory service in a large County or County Borough.

Professional training aims at producing social workers ultimately capable of holding themselves accountable for their own work; but as employees, social workers must be prepared to accept limits to their individual authority. This they are most likely to do willingly if the 'positional' authority of the administrator is democratically exercised, and recognised as being directed towards the better functioning of the social work service; and if personal and professional authority accompany it.

But the job of an administrator is different from that of a social worker, and there is no reason to suppose that a good caseworker will necessarily make a good administrator; or that the administrator need have outstanding casework skills. The social work administrator exercises authority in relation to office staff as well as social workers; and his own 'professional' authority does not derive from the same knowledge and skills as does that of the social worker – although some of these may be relevant – but depends rather on his expertise *as an administrator*. This is clearly so in the instance of the Executive of a large agency, who carries no caseload. In small agencies, and in the 'middle layers' of administration, the situation is more complex. The position of Leader of a Family Service Unit is one in which both administrative and social work skills, and authority, are demanded; and an Area Officer in a Children's Department may carry his own caseload in addition to carrying overall administrative responsibility for his area. A major problem facing agencies which are expanding, taking on additional functions, decentralising, lengthening their formal lines of communication, or appointing specialists such as Training Officers or casework 'consultants', is the clear demarcation of areas of administrative and professional authority. Correspondence also offers a practical illustration. Who is to see the letters which social workers write to their clients, and who is to sign them; and why?

2. A CLASSIFICATION OF SOCIAL WORK AGENCIES

If social work agencies have characteristics generic to them all, however, it is obvious that there are also distinguishing differences amongst them which are equally significant for

68

their administration. An attempt may now be made to classify these; although each factor identified is clearly interrelated with the others.

(a) Auspices

The broadest distinction is between statutory and voluntary agencies. The former operate under mandate from legislation with its accompanying Statutory Rules and Regulations. Their function is to serve the will of the community as expressed in legislation, as well as what social workers consider to be the needs of individual clients. For example, a Probation Order is made at the discretion not of the social worker, but of the Bench. There may be difficulty in agreeing upon an agency's primary task, if the terms of legislation in any way conflict with what social workers see as their professional function in relation to clients. Secondly, in a statutory service, major policy may originate outside the agency itself: for example, the *national* policy of integrating Prison Aftercare into the Probation Service. Thirdly, whatever kind of relationship may evolve in practice, the head of a statutory agency is technically the Executive Officer of his Committee, accountable to it for carrying out its local policy, and for seeing that its statutory obligations are met. He functions also under the sanctions of Ministry inspectorates, of tight financial control, and in the case of Children's Officers and Directors of Welfare Services, within the bureaucratic structure of Local Government.

A voluntary agency on the other hand is by definition an organisation 'initiated and governed by its own members without external control' (Bourdillon, 1945). In so far as it accepts external control, its 'voluntary' nature is diminished. Within the limits of the law, and its own capacity to raise resources, the voluntary organisation is free to decide upon its own primary task. Policy, although influenced by external events, is entirely at the discretion of the Committee; the organisational structure itself is autonomous; and the nature of the relationship between the Executive of the agency and the Committee is determined between themselves, rather than by external sanctions. (Although there are differences between organisations which are purely local, and those which have national affiliations.)

In neither statutory nor voluntary agencies however, is the Executive's 'room to manoeuvre' determined completely by such differentiating characteristics as these, but also by his response to them.

(b) Size

Size, in terms of number of staff, is an obvious differentiating factor. But simply because it is obvious, and factually incontrovertible, effects may be attributed to it which are not due to size itself, but to other factors. Anyone having experience of two similarly sized County Borough Children's Departments could produce evidence of this; and it is reasonable to suppose that differences between a City and a County Probation Department are more likely to be due to, for example, the characteristics of the areas served, than to the number of staff employed. Whereas size is logically to be identified as a differentiating factor, it is not *in itself* a very significant one. Two examples may be given of effects traditionally attributed to size, but now regarded as having other causes.

Firstly, it has tended to be assumed that the larger the organisation, the more bureaucratic it necessarily is. This is a very real issue for agencies in process of rapid expansion. An analysis of similarly sized agencies, however, might well indicate varying degrees of bureaucratisation. It is possible that the decisive factors are *administrative*: the dominant type of authority, the amount of delegation, and so on. If this is so, it means that whatever the size of the agency, the Executive can in some degree control the development of bureaucratic characteristics.

Secondly, size has traditionally resulted in longer lines of communication: in a small Children's Department, Child Care Officers will have direct access to the Children's Officer, while in a larger one the administrative hierarchy may consist of Children's Officer, Deputy Children's Officer, Senior Child Care Officer, Child Care Officers. This type of structure is rooted in the old 'scientific management' concept of 'span of control', the assumption being that there is an optimum number of staff which any one member of the executive system can effectively control. It is a pattern which dies hard. But a long vertical hierarchy with many levels of authority may not be the only way of structuring a large agency (see McGregor, 1960). If administrators are really willing to delegate authority as fully as possible, and to forego a pattern of close administrative supervision of individuals, it may be possible to devise a flat structure, with few levels of authority. The practical as well as the attitudinal problems in introducing such a policy may be considerable. Even so, it might be worth serious thought when expanding agencies are either considering introducing yet another layer into their administrative hierarchy, or increasing their administrative staff in proportion to a growing number of social workers.

(c) Complexity

Related to size, but more significant as a differentiating factor between agencies, is organisational *complexity*, due for example to multiplicity of functions, or to decentralisation.

A Children's Officer administers an agency with a variety of functions, each of them distinct, but also an integral part of the Children's Officer's overall responsibility to the Children's Committee, and of the 'organisational unit' which is the Children's Department. A department of a given size will include the provision of services by Child Care Officers, and of Residential Homes. These two functions, each with a distinct administrative structure, must be integrated into the total 'child care' function of the agency as a whole. Another Children's Department, *of similar size*, may additionally be responsible for a Remand Home, or act as an Adoption Agency, or manage an Approved School; each of these functions adding another component to be woven into the structure of the agency. The addition of a Family Casework Service to a Children's Department may not be particularly significant in so far as the number of staff employed is concerned; but it has major administrative implications because it adds another function, and thereby increases the *complexity* of the organisation. Organisations differing in size but carrying a similar range of functions may have more administrative problems in common with eath other, than with 'single function' organisations of their own size.

A second major source of organisational complexity is the number of places in which the work of the agency is done. The greater the number of residential units in a Local Authority Welfare Department or a Children's Department, the greater the range of specialisation possible, and thus the more complex the problems of ensuring that these resources are deployed efficiently in relation to the special needs of individual old people and children; and the more complex too, the problem of integrating their staff into the work of the agency as a whole. The administrative complexity im-

72

plicit in having a number of work places is perhaps revealed most clearly where there is decentralisation. Record-keeping alone offers a specific illustration: the need to reach clear decisions about what is to be duplicated between each area and central office, and between any one area and another, and in the light of these decisions to devise a system to operate uniformly in all areas.

Decentralisation tends to lead to an increase in the number of administrative staff; as for instance the introduction of Area Officers, whereas previously decisions at that particular level of authority were made by one Senior Officer only. Administratively, the core problem is that of communication. If agency policy is to be implemented uniformly in all areas, everyone must both know what it is and accept it, and the boundaries of authority must be very clearly defined. Decentralisation also introduces a centrifugal force. It diminishes the 'face to face' contact between the Executive and senior staff, and between the Executive and social workers, and calls for new methods of leadership, to ensure that allegiances are not transferred from the agency as a whole to the Area Office: that Area Officers and social workers do not become alienated from 'the administrators at Central Office'. Furthermore, problems of communication and definition of authority are horizontal in nature as well as vertical. In a decentralised Children's Department, for example, there is a possibility of a family living in one area, but the children being boarded out, or placed in a Children's Home, in another: the limit of authority of the Child Care Officer in the 'intake' area must be defined in relation to that of his counterpart in the area in which the children are placed. Problems of this nature increase the possible areas of conflict between administrative structure and good social work practice, and thus the complexity of the administrator's reconciling task.

(d) The position of social work in relation to its setting

One further differentiating factor between agencies is the position of social work in relation to the overall activities of the organisation in which it is practised.

There are agencies in which social work is the only professional service offered to clients, and in which social workers are in the direct line of communication to an agency head who, it has already been suggested, will ideally be committed to the social work function of the agency.

Within another type of agency, clients are 'shared' with other professions, and social work is only one of a range of professional disciplines which together form the basis of the agency's service to clients – as in Child Guidance Clinics, or in Local Authority Health Departments employing Medical Social Workers, Psychiatric Social Workers, or Family Caseworkers. Such agencies are not in fact social work agencies, but rather organisations in whose service to clients social work is, or may be, included, and in which the Executive's own professional commitment is not to social work. In Child Guidance Clinics, the administrative head of the agency is employed primarily in his own professional capacity (i.e. as psychiatrist or psychologist rather than as administrator), and the position of social work within the working team will be evolved on a basis of inter-professional consultation. In the more complex Health Department, the professional function of social work is less clearly defined, and social workers may expect to have to attempt to create an identity for it from the position in the hierarchy which carries the least administrative authority: the field work level.

Yet other agencies are an intrinsic part of a larger organisational unit, into which the social work administrator's authority does not extend. Such are Social Work Departments of hospitals. Here too clients are 'shared' with other professions, but in this case with professions in a separate authority system from the Social Work Department itself. Major administrative problems will centre round those issues of social work significance which cannot be broached unless the Senior Medical Worker has access through a clear line of communication to those points in the administrative structure of the hospital at which relevant decisions can be made.

Finally, at this stage in the development of social work training, it may be relevant to single out for special consideration social *service* agencies which are in process of becoming social *work* agencies, such as Local Authority Welfare Departments. As the Younghusband courses begin to feed trained social workers into such departments, a new dimension will be added to the social service function of providing material amenities such as Part III accommodation or household aids for the handicapped. The sanctioning legislation may remain unchanged, but the method of implementing it will alter, and with it the relationship between administrative and specialist staff.

To summarise, agencies differ from each other in the auspices under which they operate, in size, in complexity, and in the status and position of social work in relation to its administrative environment. These are factors with which each social work administrator is confronted in his own particular setting. On the other hand, all agencies also have certain characteristics in common. They are alike in that their primary task is to produce services not goods; in that their work is rooted in a shared system of values; and in that the relationship between administrative and professional authority is in all of them important. These are characteristics which call for some degree of specialisation in the administration of social work agencies as distinct from organisations of other kinds, and which give to social work administration its own 'generic' identity.

V

Social work administration

The focus henceforward will be on the social work administrator's specific contribution to the agency's work. His equipment, it has already been suggested, must include an appreciation of the nature of the organisation of which he is a part, and with and through which he must work; and a brief recapitulation of some of the major points already made may precede the analysis of his tasks:

As an *organisation*, an agency:

(i) Has a formal structure: a set of positions through which members relate to each other 'officially'.

(ii) Is a social unit, composed of individuals whose inter-relationships are not exclusively official, but also personal.

(iii) Was created to serve particular purposes; but may also develop other objectives.

(iv) Cannot exist independently of the world outside it, but is organically linked to its environment.

(v) Is subject to continuous change, whether planned or unplanned.

(vi) Both owns and requires resources for the work it has to do.

As a *social work* organisation, an agency:

(i) Has the primary task of producing services for people.

(ii) Owes allegiance to social work values.

(iii) May differ from other agencies by virtue of its auspices, its size, its complexity, or the position of the social work element in it in relation to the whole.

Within such an 'organisational' context must the social work administrator organise resources to get work effectively done. It may be re-emphasised that his main concern is with the relationship between people and work; and that leadership, decision-making, communication, and the exercise of authority are major components of his activity.

With these concepts as a background, this chapter will consider the position of the administrator within the agency, the broader aspects of his function, and the roles which he carries; preliminary to the discussion in Chapter VI of specific components of the administrative task.

I. THE POSITION OF THE SOCIAL WORK ADMINISTRATOR

The social work administrator does his job from a fixed position in the agency's formal structure. As head of an agency he is, except for his relationship to the employing body, at the apex of this structure; as a Senior Officer, at some intermediate point in the hierarchy. The position which an administrator fills in relation to other positions is in practice a correlate of his authority – that is of his power to make effective decisions. The 'official' position of every agency member may be indicated on an organisation chart; but such a chart reveals nothing of how these positions relate to each other in practice. For example, one set of positions in a Children's Department might be illustrated thus:

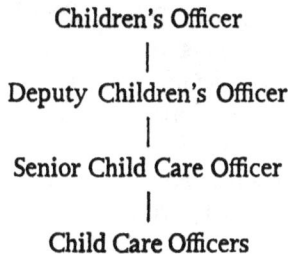

Children's Officer

|

Deputy Children's Officer

|

Senior Child Care Officer

|

Child Care Officers

If, however, the Children's Officer 'keeps an open door', and Child Care Officers approach him direct, what is the effect on the intermediate positions of the Senior and the Deputy? Positions can be accurately defined only in terms of the effective authority vested in them; or, alternatively, as points in a system of communication. In the illustration given, the Senior Child Care Officer's position looks clear on paper, but disappears in practice. Similarly, an organisation chart may indicate a super/subordinate relationship between an Area Officer and his 'superior' at Central Office. But unless the limits of authority of each are clearly defined, i.e. unless it is clear what decisions are to be made by whom, their positions on a chart will be without a practical counterpart. The same is true of positions which stand in a 'horizontal' relationship to each other, e.g. Chief Administrative Officer – Senior Child Care Officer – Training Officer – Senior Family Caseworker. To set out these positions thus on paper, does not tell how in practice they interlock, or overlap, or conflict.

The position of the administrator, as of every agency member, must be defined in terms of the limits of his own authority in relation to that of the holders of other positions. A recent advertisement sought a Senior Child Care Officer 'to undertake the usual duties of a Senior'. What, however, are the usual duties of a Senior? And what will be the position in the agency of a Senior Officer whose duties are not in fact more clearly defined than this?

The position of an agency head is clear inasmuch as he is the ultimate source of authority; although if he is imprecise in his delegation of authority, he will blur the outlines of both his own position, and those of his subordinates. Positions are created by the delegation of authority, and the position of Senior Child Care Officer referred to in the advertisement has no meaning until it is defined in terms of the precise authority to be vested in it *in that one particular agency.*

It follows that although every organisation by definition has a formal structure, this is not immutably fixed, but is amenable to change according to the way in which duties are distributed. It is a matter in which the Executive can exercise a certain degree of choice; and the choices he makes in locating a new position will have major implications for the agency as a working unit.

One example may illustrate this point. If it has been decided to appoint a Family Caseworker to a decentralised Children's Department with three Area Offices, there are a variety of ways in which his duties can be defined and his position be located in the formal structure. The administrative problem is to correlate the two. If he is to work exclusively as a member of the social work team in one area only, then it would be appropriate for him to derive his authority from (i.e. be responsible to) the Area Officer concerned, and his position might be illustrated thus:

Children's Officer
|
Deputy Children's Officer
|

Area Officer   Area Officer   Area Officer
|

Family   Child Care   Child Care   Child Care
Caseworker Officers   Officers   Officers

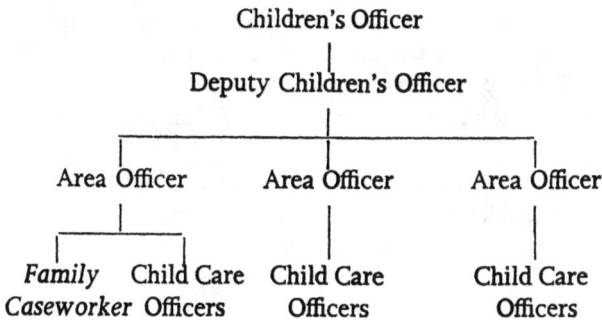

If on the other hand, it is intended that he shall not himself carry a caseload, but act as a consultant in respect of families needing intensive help *irrespective of area*, then the limits of his authority must be defined in relation to *each* Area Officer. In the next figure, he is placed in a 'horizontal' relationship to all three of them. Like them he is responsible to the Deputy Children's Officer; and his authority in relation to them will be a function of his professional competence: it will be 'specialist' authority, and not 'administrative' (see Chapter III, 2 c).

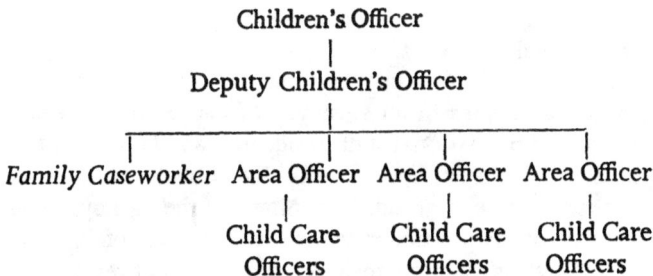

Children's Officer
|
Deputy Children's Officer
|

Family Caseworker   Area Officer   Area Officer   Area Officer
|

Child Care   Child Care   Child Care
Officers   Officers   Officers

As well as requiring the definition of job-content, the creation of a new position has implications for an agency's

81

salary structure. And it will raise questions concerning the status which colleagues are prepared to ascribe to it; for even 'official' positions are not contained entirely within the formal structure, but provoke personal attitudes and feelings.

Having looked at some of the attributes of any position, we may consider in more detail the position of the Executive, and then of senior administrators responsible to him.

(a) The position of the executive

Four dimensions of the Executive's position are particularly significant:

(i) *His position within the agency*. In this position is vested administrative responsibility for agency operation. It is the ultimate source of authority and of appeal; and in the formal communication system it is a unique source, and repository, of information. One of its most important characteristics is its uniqueness: at the apex of the agency's formal structure. It is a lonely position: for to whatever extent an Executive may involve his staff in decision-making processes, the responsibility for decisions reached remains his; and there are decisions which he must be prepared to make alone. There is a further way in which the uniqueness of his position sets him apart. Splits may appear between groupings in an agency, as for example between clerical and professional staff, residential and field staff, the trained and the untrained. The Executive's position is attached to no one group. Committed to the agency, he is by virtue of his position detached from it; part of it, he is enabled by his position to look at it in its entirety.

(ii) *His position in relation to employers*. Like all other agency members, the Executive is an employee. But again his position is unique, in that it is the one formal link in the line of communication between the agency and the employing body. The position of the Head Medical Social Worker in relation to the Hospital Management Committee obviously differs from that of the Principal Probation Officer in relation to the Probation Committee, in a number of important ways. Whatever the nature of the relationship however, it is only through this one position that formal communication on matters concerning the agency as a whole can be maintained.

Furthermore, whereas the position of the Executive is *super*ordinate in relation to all other employees, in relation to his employers it is subordinate: he too in this important respect is at an intermediate position in the hierarchy.

(iii) *His position in relation to other controlling bodies.* In any statutory setting where the primary function is social work, the position of the Executive links the agency not only to employers, but to the Government Department through which Ministerial responsibility is met. Although technically a Ministry exercises authority through the relevant local committee, the crucial position is that of the committee's Executive; for it is through this that Ministry requirements are in fact met, and that the quality of central/local relationships is developed.

(iv) *His position in relation to the community.* Every social worker is a link between agency and community, as represented for example by clients or other agencies. But the position of the Executive is the unique formal point of reference between the agency as a whole and the world outside it. As he faces 'inward' in relation to agency members, so he faces 'outward' to the community, as the agency's representative. Thus 'the Children's Officer' or 'the Principal Probation Officer' will in a variety of situations be the embodiment of the agency itself. Additionally, the Executive's position corresponds to that of other agency Executives, and he alone relates to them as peers. For this reason, it may be through his position only that matters of inter-agency policy can be raised.

To sum up, the Executive's position in relation to other members of the agency, to the employing body, to other controlling bodies, and to the community, demands of him and makes possible to him, behaviour which is appropriate to him alone. In comparison, we may look very briefly at the position of the Senior Officer.

(b) *The position of the senior officer*

It is probably in Children's Departments that intermediate layers in the administrative hierarchy are at present most extensively found; but Probation Departments too have Senior Officers, Tutor Officers, and sometimes Training Officers. Any such reorganisation of the personal social services of the Local Authority as is anticipated in the recent White Paper (Home Office, 1965) might be expected to lead to an increase in the size and complexity of the administrative units in which social workers are employed, and key positions in Local Authority social work services seem likely to be increasingly in what in industry would be called 'middle management'. Every position in an agency is subject to pressure from at least two directions, eg.:

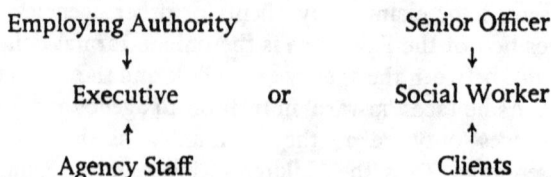

Employing Authority		Senior Officer
↓		↓
Executive	or	Social Worker
↑		↑
Agency Staff		Clients

The Senior Officer is somewhere in the middle of the line of authority from Executive to social worker. His position is part of the executive system : but one of its characteristics is that it is subject to *administrative* pressure from above, and *professional* pressure from below:

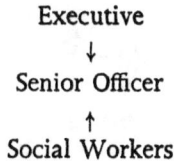

Executive

↓

Senior Officer

↑

Social Workers

For both the Executive and the Senior Officer, his position in the organisation is significant for the work he has to do. It is unwise to assume that personality is the only determinant of an administrator's behaviour: for what he is able to do is determined also by his position in the structure of the agency (Simon, 1961).

2. THE FUNCTION OF THE SOCIAL WORK ADMINISTRATOR

In his particular position, the administrator performs his administrative function. This is not to do the work of the agency, but to maintain the agency in operation. The fact that the administrator's job is *different* from that of the social worker demands a major adjustment on the part of those who move from social work to administrative positions. In some situations, administrative and specialist functions may be appropriately combined in one position. The Head Medical Social Worker for example may carry a caseload simply because the agency does not need her full-time services as an administrator. In other situations, however, administrators may be carrying case-loads either because they are for personal reasons reluctant to relinquish their social work roles; or because their administrative positions have not been adequately defined, and they have not been able to identify for themselves an administrative function which they feel to be of value. This function consists of keeping the agency 'in good working order', and includes:

(i) *Formulating the agency's objectives.* An agency head is the executive officer of his employers, responsible for implementing their policy decisions. Although broad terms of reference are drawn from legislation or constitution, it is only through administrative processes that policy can be given systematic expression, and that an agency can be given a corporative sense of direction. For example, the Local Authority is required by legislation to provide for children in care in such a way as to further their best interests (Children Act, 1948). But what can this mean, apart from the objectives which are formulated by the Children's Officer in relation to such questions as the closing down of Cottage Homes; or the recruitment of trained social work staff; or the payment of special rates to foster parents taking 'difficult' children; or experiments with new social work methods such as group work; and so on? In formulating objectives such as these, the Executive is devising methods by which the function of the agency can be implemented. In so far as new objectives require committee sanction, he is also contributing to the formulation of policy; and his relationship with his committee becomes not exclusively executive, but also advisory. He is concerned not just with the here and now, but with the future. In the last resort, the vitality of an agency depends extensively on the sensitivity of the Executive to stimulus from the agency's changing environment; and his function of formulating objectives is a continuing one.

(ii) *The provision of a formal structure* to serve as an effective communication system. The significance of the administrator's own position has already been discussed, and it has been stressed that the positions of members of staff in relation to each other can be *planned*. The position used to illustrate this was that of a Family Caseworker; but the same applies to any position in the agency, whether administrative, or social work, or residential, or clerical. Whereas overall responsibility for agency structure rests with the Executive, within the limits of his own authority – e.g. an Area Office – a Senior Officer must perform a similar planning function.

(iii) *The promotion of co-operative effort.* As already seen, an agency consists not only of a formal structure, but of a social system composed of individuals. As individuals join organisations, including social work agencies, for their own personal reasons, their nominal membership is an inadequate basis for full participation in the work of the agency as a co-operating unit. The administrator's function is to attempt to lessen the conflict between the needs of the agency as an organisation, and the separate needs of its individual members; and to enhance that widespread sense of commitment to the agency, whether of social workers or clerks, which constitutes high morale. The 1965 White Paper supplies an example of a situation in which this particular administrative function could be of special significance, in suggesting that in the event of legislation, social workers might be recruited to the proposed Children's Service from the Probation and Aftercare Service (Home Office, 1965). Probation Officers, it would probably be agreed, meet some of their own individual needs through the exercise of the authority vested in them by the Probation Order, and the responsibility which they feel free to assume in relation to their 'own' probationers. Children in care, however, do not 'belong' to individual Child Care Officers in this way: it is the Local Authority which assumes parental rights, or is named in the Fit Person Order, and the authority for taking a child into care under Section I of the Children Act is vested in the Children's Officer. Probation Officers transferring to a Children's Department would find themselves in situations in which the agency makes demands on them which, while not necessarily restrictive in themselves, might seem so because they are part of an authority system different from that to which the Probation Officer is accustomed. The 'integrating' function of the Executive would have considerable demands made upon it.

(iv) *Finding and deploying resources.* To do its work, an agency needs resources – human, material, and time. The common denominator is money, adequate not only to maintain standards, but for development. The direct responsibility which the Executive takes for money raising will depend on the nature of the agency. In a voluntary agency, for example, the assumption of this responsibility by the committee can usefully free the Executive for the performance of his other functions.

The most significant attribute of resources is that they tend to be a reflection of policy. Poor interviewing or waiting-room accommodation, or the continued predominance of untrained staff, may be symptomatic of the Executive's attitude towards these matters. We have already seen that his function includes participation in policy formulation; and he must attempt to translate new legislative provisions, for example, or new ideas on residential accommodation for children, or unmet needs in the community, or new social work methods, into terms of the resources needed to implement them; and make a case to the employing body for the recruitment of such resources. He must respond to emergent needs within the agency – for extra staff, or accommodation, or foster parents, or voluntary workers – and assume responsibility for attempting to meet them. Whether or not these needs are met may not ultimately rest with him. But he must represent the agency and its needs at the appropriate points; and his willingness to do this may in itself help to relieve staff of some of the pressure which working with inadequate resources causes them to feel.

Resources once obtained have to be deployed: a process which demands the making of choices and the selection of priorities, and is thus inherent in the formulation and implementation of policy, and in the administrative function of making the agency efficient in the performance of its task.

Authority itself may be defined in terms of control over resources. The Executive's authority is a correlate of his control over the total resources of the agency; and when he delegates authority, what he is in fact delegating is the power to use resources. For example, he delegates to senior officers authority over the way in which social workers (human resources) use their skills and their time.

Control over resources must be commensurate with the work to be done: it is only under this condition that an individual can rationally be held accountable for the performance of his task. With an excessive caseload, for example, a social worker commands an inappropriate amount of time; with a particularly difficult case, a young and untrained worker may command an inadequate degree of skill; without control of a specified amount of the time of untrained workers, a training officer may not properly be held accountable for the implementation of an in-service training programme.

Every agency member controls resources which are personal to him as well as belonging to the agency, e.g. his skills. The administrator, at whatever level in the hierarchy, controls resources external to himself. He carries responsibility as an administrator for deploying them efficiently in pursuit of the agency's purposes, and for identifying and acting upon the need to increase them.

(v) *Supervision and evaluation.* If his functions in relation to objectives, policy, and resources indicate the administrator's responsibility towards the agency's future, he is also accountable for its present performance, and must *oversee* its activities. The word 'oversee' has, as suggested in Chapter I, unpleasant connotations. It is used here deliberately, for the problems associated with staff supervision are not to be overcome by denying that this particular administrative function exists, but rather by discovering how it can be used to the advantage of both the staff member and the agency, and thus of clients.

The exercise of administrative authority in relation to subordinates may be an uncomfortable activity for social work administrators because:

(*a*) Feelings about authority carried over from their former social work roles may make its active exercise distasteful.

(*b*) They may on promotion be called upon to supervise social workers who were formerly their peers.

(*c*) Staff supervision is thought to reflect adversely on the competence and status of social work members of staff.

(*d*) Social workers may resent supervision of their work; and social work administrators see no justification for it.

(*e*) Administrators may doubt their own competence to supervise those social workers whose social work skills they may consider to equal or surpass their own.

It is again relevant to emphasise that the administrator's job is *different* from that of the social worker; and that it is his task to ensure that agency purposes are fulfilled. He need not be a 'better' social worker than those he supervises, for his function is not to do social work, but to help social workers to function more effectively *as agency members*. As an administrator, he has the supervisory function of allocating work, and of seeing that it is done, and how it is done. The exercise of this function is essential to the agency as a working unit; for the implementation of policy and the efficient use of resources both require that the individual be held accountable for both what he does, and how he does it. Neither the administrator nor the social worker can separate out exclusively 'professional' from exclusively 'administrative' elements in supervision. Consultation, in the sense of the social worker being left free to ask for advice when he feels that he needs it, leaves out of account both the administrator's responsibility for standards of work, and the social worker's role not as 'social worker' only, but as employee.

Another dimension of staff supervision however, is the 'staff development' function. Resistance to the idea of staff supervision in this country is widespread; and the concept of staff *evaluation* is probably so new as to have received little consideration. But unless it is assumed that supervision and evaluation as methods of improving skills lose their value automatically when a student 'qualifies' and becomes a member of staff, there is a useful function for both from the point of view of the individual social worker who wishes to continue to improve his practice. The social work administrator exercises 'oversight' – and authority – on behalf of the agency; but intrinsic to administrative supervision is the development of individual competence. A social worker's skills belong both to himself and to the agency; and their development through supervision and evaluation provides a nice example of the administrative task of reconciling organisational and individual needs.

Furthermore, administrative supervision and evaluation apply not only in respect of individual social workers, but to the total performance of that part of the agency for which any particular administrator carries responsibility. The value of his activities in relation particularly to agency objectives, but also to agency structure, the promotion of co-operative effort, and the recruitment and deployment of resources, will be dissipated unless the performance of the agency as a working unit is subject to continuous scrutiny: for this only can keep it on course.

3. THE ROLE OF THE SOCIAL WORK ADMINISTRATOR

We have considered some implications of the administrator's position, and suggested a broad framework of functional responsibilities. But a further dimension of both his position and his function is the way in which he *perceives himself* in his administrative capacity, and the way in which he *is perceived* by others: for the former will help to determine the way in which he in fact behaves, and the latter the behaviour which is expected of him.

Each member of an agency is assigned to a status, which is to say a collection of duties and rights (Linton, 1963), and may be said to occupy the status of, for example, Probation Officer, or housemother, or receptionist. An individual may leave the agency, but unless the content of the job is redefined, his successor will inherit the same status – the same duties and rights. The status is the same whoever occupies it, and what differs is the way in which different individuals put the status into effect: that is, the way in which they perform their *roles*. The impact of the individual on a particular status is clearly felt when an agency acquires a new Executive. The duties of a Principal Probation Officer, for example, are formally described in the Probation Rules, but each new Principal will have his own perception of how they should be implemented, and staff will wait with some uncertainty to see how the new-comer interprets his role.

The way in which each incumbent of a position perceives his own role and that of others, and the way in which they perceive his, vitally affects relationships. For example, if the Executive has one conception of his role, and an Area Officer another, they cannot work effectively together. The individual will be free of conflict only when he has clarified his own role, and feels that he is conforming to it, and when his interpretation of it is clear to his colleagues.

The need for clarity can perhaps best be illustrated from the case of social workers who are promoted to administrative positions. Here they are being assigned to a different status, with a different role. Discomfort felt in this new status may to no small extent be due to confusion over roles. The new administrator may be clear neither about the status of his new position – that is about the rights and duties which go with it; nor about the expectations which others have of him. The role he knows best is that of social worker; and if he has been promoted within the agency, his former peers may themselves be confused as to what to expect of him in the new situation. Unless his new role is made explicit, they may tend to continue to view him primarily as a social worker, and to expect of him qualities and activities which are appropriate to a social worker rather than to an administrator.

The situation is further complicated by the fact that individuals in an agency occupy more than one status, such as for example both social worker and court officer; and also because the way in which they define their multiple roles, and distinguish between them, is a function of their total personality, including the roles they carry outside the agency. The administrator, like the social worker, occupies the status of employee, but also that of supervisor, and possibly of subordinate; of colleague; and of member of a professional social work association; and if he also carries a caseload, that of social worker. He needs to distinguish between these roles, and to identify the behaviour appropriate to each of them: to be able to say to himself 'as a social worker I might act or feel like this, but as an administrator I carry a different role, and therefore my behaviour must be different'.

Finally, the status of the administrator involves not only performance of a role *vis-à-vis* superiors, subordinates, and peers, but also a complement of other relationships. As we have already seen, the Executive of an agency holds a position in relation not only to agency employees, but to the employing authority, to peers in other agencies, and to representatives of other groups in the community. Comparably, within the hospital itself, a head medical social worker carries an administrative role in relation to the hospital secretary, consultants, ward sisters, medical auxiliaries, and so on. Sociologists would call this collection of relationships deriving from a status a 'role set'. The concept is potentially useful for the administrator; for part of his effectiveness will depend on the extent to which he is able clearly to identify and implement those 'role relationships' which are of significance for the promotion of the agency's purpose.

The concept of role is familiar to social workers, as a means of 'differentiating aspects of a person's behaviour, feelings, and ideas, and for linking them in a meaningful way to those of other significant people in his environment' (Timms, 1962). Like the concept of authority discussed in Chapter III, 'role' is a concept as relevant to administration as it is to social work.

VI

Social work administration—(continued)

The function of the administrator, it has been suggested, is to provide an agency with a well-designed formal structure; to promote co-operative effort among its members; to find and deploy resources; and to direct, manage, supervise, and evaluate the agency's performance. Incidental to this broadly stated function is a range of activities which this chapter will attempt to classify. For the sake of brevity, the focus will be on the agency Executive, but other administrators, each in accordance with his own particular context, have a participating function. In some of the activities to be identified, such as staff supervision, the tasks of the 'senior' will derive from his 'administrative' or 'executive' authority in relation to subordinates; in others, such as staff recruitment, the senior may carry an *advisory* role, in relation to the head of the agency.

Because the agency is an organic whole, none of the activities in which the Executive participates can be logically separated off from the others. Staff recruitment and in-service training for example are inter-related; and budgeting is a denominator common to them both. The following classification thus attempts nothing more than a broad grouping.

(a) Staffing

Because the agency's major resources are human, activities in relation to staffing form the core of the administrator's task; and in even the smallest agency, the Executive must perform tasks which might in an industrial concern be the function of a personnel manager.

(i) *Recruitment.* Even within the same social service, there is considerable variation in the part which the employing authority plays in the recruitment of social workers (Kammerer, 1962); and in some agencies typists may be engaged directly by the Executive as employees of the agency, whereas in other cases they may be engaged, and deployed, by a central Establishments Officer. Thus the 'staffing' tasks of the Executive will be affected by factors such as the nature of his formal relationship with his employers. Nevertheless, whatever the context, they are to be seen as integral to his broader functions in respect of policy, agency structure, and resources. And whatever may be the limitations of the executive authority vested in him, he in any case has an advisory role to perform.

In the sphere of employment policy, the onus is on the Executive to use to the full, and perhaps to extend, his scope in helping both to formulate and to implement a policy designed to improve the quality of the service which the agency is attempting to give. He must be prepared to reach conclusions on questions such as these: What are the minimum social work qualifications acceptable to the agency? Can, or should, the agency wait until it can fill vacant positions with trained workers? What levels of training and skill are needed for any positions which have to be filled, social work or other? If untrained newcomers are to be recruited, what ought to be provided in the way of in-service training? Within the scope available to it, what is to be the agency's salary policy? What special financial rewards can it offer for special qualifications and experience? How best can it set about recruiting the type of worker it needs; and how best can it encourage him to stay? What facilities can it offer for 'staff development'? Why do people leave?

This list of questions may appear somewhat arbitrary. The essence of it is that these are not questions to be considered separately on an 'ad hoc' basis, but are integral to the formulation of a recruitment *policy*, directed to building up a stable and effective 'labour force', and calling for consistent action in relation to recruitment, salary structure, in-service training, and promotion.

(ii) *Selection*. In the light of general employment policy, the Executive has the task of ensuring that staff is wisely selected. He must see that the job to be done is clearly defined, for as already suggested, it is this which will determine the formal position of the newcomer in relation to colleagues. He must clarify the qualifications and skills which the job demands. And he must recognise that he is selecting not only a 'typist' or a 'social worker', with the necessary typing skills or social work qualifications, but also a person who will be a member of his working group, and who will bring to the agency his own needs and aspirations.

(iii) *Staff development*. Employment policy like all other aspects of administration, is concerned with the future: and one aspect of this is the development of the skills which newcomers bring with them to the agency. The social work administrator has a commitment in this respect not only to his own agency, but to social work as a whole. Induction

97

arrangements for new members of staff; a programme of in-service training; regular supervision; staff meetings; encouragement and assistance for attendance at part-time or refresher courses; and secondment for full-time training, are all methods of attempting to promote the effectiveness of the agency. Ideally they derive also from the responsibility of the social work administrator to contribute to the development of social work skills in general, and from a responsibility to his staff as individuals with a potential for growth. Administratively, they presuppose an assumption that continued education is important enough to merit an allocation of agency time.

(iv) *Promotion.* Staff development implies the existence of a promotion policy. The scope available to an agency Executive will be determined in part by such factors as the size and complexity of the agency; the degree of autonomy held by the employing authority; the extent to which salary scales are determined on a national rather than a local basis; and the differing functions assumed by professional organisations, such as the National Association of Probation Officers compared with the Association of Child Care Officers. Theoretically, the basic task of the Executive is to determine, within the scope for differentiation open to him, a distribution of duties and rewards which will afford the fullest opportunity for individuals to exercise their developing potential, and at the same time provide an attractive career structure. In practice, the existing structure of the social services leaves him small room to manoeuvre.

The overall problem of a career structure in social work will be presented in the next chapter as relevant to any restructuring of the statutory social work services. Within his own agency, however, the Executive can at least attempt to work in accordance with sound administrative principles.

He may need for example to recognise the point at which the conflict between organisational and individual needs cannot be resolved within the agency, and at which he must bless the individual in his attempts to seek promotion elsewhere, rather than encourage him to stay. An example of a failure to recognise a situation of this kind may be given from a Children's Department in which a Child Care Officer was 'promoted' to a 'senior' position in order to discourage her from leaving. Her salary was increased and her title was changed, but she continued in practice to do the work of a Child Care Officer. Her own need for an opportunity to carry increased responsibility remained unmet, and her colleagues resented the increase in salary unaccompanied by a corresponding change in function. In another instance, a Training Officer promoted from a social work position had his salary increased and his new title announced several months before the new position became 'operational'. The interim period was one of considerable discomfort, during which neither he nor his colleagues could clarify his role.

(v) *Welfare*. In industry, the concept of employee welfare has been bedevilled by conflicting theories about the effects of welfare services on morale and on productivity. In social work administration, by virtue of the 'service' character of agencies, and the value system of social work, it is reasonable to hope that concern for the 'welfare' of members of staff will derive from the value which the Executive attaches to them simply as people, irrespective of whether or not there is any correlation between well-being and efficiency in the individual employee. There may nevertheless be a dilemma of a different kind, familiar already to the social work supervisor; and it is important to stress that it is not part of the 'welfare' task of the administrator to act as a caseworker for staff. Here again

99

the concept of 'role' may be useful. The roles of the administrator and the caseworker are different, and the role of the administrator in relation to staff welfare is to be seen as deriving from his function of promoting co-operation within the agency and, in so far as this is possible, of integrating the needs of individual and organisation without damage to either. Yet as the role of the caseworker is limited by the function of the agency, so the role of the administrator in relation to members of staff is limited by the employment situation of which all are part.

Nevertheless, although congenial physical conditions, flexible working hours, and any 'fringe benefits' may reflect an Executive's interest in the general comfort of his staff – as well as his concern to minimise turnover – the welfare of any individual within an organisation demands a more sophisticated use than this of an administrator's human skills. In a recent pamphlet, Lupton (1964) suggests that in organisations as elsewhere, 'welfare' includes the satisfaction of the needs which individuals feel 'to be recognised, to be esteemed and well regarded, to be cared about'. Mary Follett postulates that it is part of the task of the administrator to help others to participate in his leadership: to 'know how to create a *group power* rather than to express a personal power' (Metcalf, 1941). McGregor sees a task for the administrator in the extension of the scope which the organisation gives to the individual for the exercise of his own creativity and of his intellectual potential (McGregor, 1960). If these propositions are accepted, then it is indeed not as a caseworker that the executive must see his 'welfare' task; for it becomes an integral part of the administrative process of getting the organisation's work well done.

To summarise what has been said so far, recruitment policy and selection, staff development, promotion policy, and welfare, are component parts of the Executive's task of *staffing* the agency. A second task involves him in responsibilities reaching beyond the agency itself, i.e.:

(b) Student training

Fieldwork placements have of course been an integral part of training for social work since the very beginning, and working relationships have typically been established between course tutors and those members of agencies who act as student supervisors, with students themselves forming the third corner of the triangle. Like staff supervision however, student training has an administrative dimension as well as an educational one, and however willing the student supervisor, it is only with the active co-operation of the Executive that student training can be effectively incorporated into agency policy and practice.

The Executive's task in relation to student training might be summarised as to give leadership, and to allocate resources. The leadership which he gives will depend on the sense of commitment to social work as a method of implementing a social service, which has already been suggested as an essential ingredient of social work administration. This commitment may extend in practice to social work as a profession, or to social work of a particular type, or in a particular social service. The Principal Probation Officer, for example, may be called upon to decide where he stands in relation to requests from Home Office courses for placements for students in training for the Probation Service, and from Universities for placements either for those who are already committed to other fields, or who are undecided. On the nature of the Executive's commitment, and on its place in his scale of priorities, will depend the formulation of an agency *policy* in relation to student training, including a move away from a situation in which an agency may 'fit a student in' as and when it can, to one in which it becomes established practice for it to accept students from particular courses on a regularised basis.

The basic administrative task in relation to student training lies thus in the area of policy making. Aligned with this is the task of policy implementation. This demands the recruitment and allocation of resources, in this instance for an activity which carries no assurance of measurable returns to the agency. It is part of the Executive's task to assess what resources are needed, to weigh them in the balance with other demands, and in the light of his conclusions, to assume such sponsorship for them as he considers they require.

Student training draws on human resources, material resources, and time, and on their common denominator which is money. It demands the allocation of human resources in the form, for example, of supervisory skills. It demands material resources in the form of, for example, office accommodation. It demands the allocation of time; and thus calls for decisions about the size of caseload appropriate for a social worker who is also supervising students, or about the appointment of a full time student supervisor. It calls also for the clarification of the position and role of supervisors of students within the agency, for one of their essential resources will be the support and co-operation of colleagues.

Whatever the professional quality of the tutor-supervisor-student relationship, the Executive must see, and help others to see, that the triangle is rooted in the agency, as part of the administrative process.

(c) Property and equipment

A further category of administrative tasks are those which

the Americans would neatly classify as 'housekeeping': the tasks concerned with providing and maintaining the material resources which the agency needs. The administrative significance of the 'housekeeping' task of the Executive is multidimensional.

Firstly, the physical conditions under which a service is given tend to be a reflection of significant values. Pleasant waiting room accommodation implies respect for those who have to use it; privacy for interviews indicates a regard for the dignity of the client, and for the professional nature of the social work relationship; the adequacy or otherwise of recording equipment or of transport may reflect the value set upon social workers' time; space set apart for students indicates something of the way in which the agency defines its responsibility to them; and the type of accommodation provided for residential staff in Children's Homes may indicate an attempt to balance the needs of members of staff for privacy, with the needs of the children for access to them.

Secondly, because property and equipment cost money, their acquisition and maintenance call for decisions as to priorities – in relation both to any expenditure over which the Executive has direct control, and to expenditure for which he must seek the sanction of his employers. Some of these decisions may be an integral part of long term policy planning. For example, a policy of decentralisation may be considered desirable in a County Children's Department on the grounds that a 'preventive' service must be easily accessible to potential clients; but such a policy cannot be implemented without the making of decisions as to what type of accommodation will be needed, and how much of it, and where.

Thirdly, the day to day management and use of property and equipment has to be built into the administrative structure of the agency. Office space and cars, telephones, filing cabinets and dictaphones, are all most appropriately to be regarded as equipment of which the adequate supply and orderly use are essential if the agency is to profit to the full from the human resources available to it.

(d) Budgeting

In a large agency, the processes of preparing and presenting an annual budget have technical aspects which are generic to accountancy rather than to social work. The intention of this introduction to administration, however, has been to present social work administration as having the primary task of promoting the social work function of the agency; and if the point holds good for any of the administrative tasks already outlined, it is no less valid in respect of budgeting.

All too often, the Annual Report of a voluntary agency will confine the presentation of accounts to a statement of expenditure during the year under review, in fulfilment of its statutory duty to make such information public, and supporters of the agency may be content to read what has already been spent, rather than to demand a precise statement concerning the year to come. The private agency in the United States, on the other hand, if it depends for its income on an annual grant from the Community Chest, has to meet the challenge of presenting a request for a specific amount of money, and of showing specifically how the money would be spent.

The Executive of a Local Authority department faces a comparable situation in that he is required annually to prepare for the Local Authority, and to justify, a statement of estimated expenditure for the coming year. In preparing his estimates, the Executive is concerned with ensuring for the agency the resources which will be needed if policy is to be transplanted into practice. The task is one which he will share with his committee; and which is carried out not exclusively in the confines of the agency, but within the Local Government environment in which the agency is embedded. Its successful performance will require, on the one hand, clear thinking about the developing objectives of the agency, about the resources which will be needed to implement them, about the nature of those choices between alternatives which a scarcity of resources always requires; and, on the other hand, it will require the technical skill needed to steer a course through the complex structure of Local Government finance.

A budget inevitably represents a compromise between the desirable and the possible; and from the administrative as distinct from the accountancy point of view, its significance is that it is a statement of the agency's intended programme – translated into fiscal terms. The preparation of estimates, and the process of 'getting them through', incidentally serve the purpose of forcing the Executive to think ahead in terms of the future programme of the agency, and of the resources which will be needed to carry it out. The budget is one device by which the Executive may be held accountable for the use of resources; and it is also a device which he himself can use in the implementation of his administrative function of evaluating the agency's performance in relation to the resources available to it. The nature of his direct responsibility for 'fund raising' will vary considerably from one type of agency to another: but the relationship between policy planned and revenue needed must everywhere be his concern.

(e) *A records system*

A function of the Executive discussed in Chapter V, is to

provide the agency with a formal structure to serve as a communication system. So far, this communication system has been considered primarily as a network of positions; but an essential correlate of it is a records system. Records are a mechanism through which the activities of individuals may be related in an orderly way to the needs and purposes of the agency, and individuals themselves be provided with what might best be described as a map of the agency's activities.

Case-recording, for example, serves a professional purpose as a method used by the social worker for the analysis of the worker/client relationship. But even the case-record, perhaps the most 'personalised' form of record there is, belongs not to the social worker but to the agency, reflecting the fact that it is only his membership of the agency which sanctions his access to the client in the first place. Whatever purpose the case-record serves for the worker, it is also a means of ensuring continuity, for the agency's service to the client must be maintained, even if individual workers leave. Furthermore, case-recording is one of the devices by which the social worker may be held accountable for the quality of his work. Case-records may be used as part of the internal agency processes of supervision and evaluation; or, as in the Probation Service, their compulsory completion may be a means whereby the social worker is held responsible for the performance of his statutory functions. Thus even this most individual type of record performs functions for the agency as well as for the individual social worker; and its quality is a matter of administrative as well as of professional significance.

Some records are kept because the employing or statutory authority require it; but this apart, the establishment and maintenance of an efficient internal record system is an administrative responsibility of the Executive. In principle, firstly he must reach decisions as to what must be put down in writing, and what can safely be left to be carried in people's heads; secondly, having decided what must be recorded, he must decide how it is to be recorded, and by whom; thirdly, he must ensure that access to recorded information is easily accessible to those who need it for the performance of their specialist functions.

A records system is justifiable only if it is useful: and if it is seen to serve the purposes of making the agency as a whole more efficient, whether in terms of service to clients or of the prompt payment of mileage allowances to individuals, members of staff can justifiably be held accountable for operating it. And if it is the task of the Executive to ensure that an effective records system is devised, maintained, and if necessary altered to meet changing circumstances, it is no less the duty of the social worker, as an agency member, to accept administrative responsibility for his own share in implementing it.

(f) Public relations

It has already been emphasised that agencies are not self-contained units but are linked to their environment, and that the Executive holds a position which places him in a particular relationship to the outside world, whether this be conceived of as the agency's immediate setting, or the local community.

On a variety of occasions, the Executive is the agency's official representative, as a member of the Co-ordinating committee, for example, or in formal contacts with the Executives of other agencies. But in addition to performing the specific task in hand, he is also giving expression to a relationship between his own agency and those with whom he is carrying out its business. On such occasions he not only represents the agency, but to all intents and purposes *is* the agency, and on him falls ultimate responsibility for creating its 'public image'.

No agency functions in isolation. It is at the centre of a series of concentric circles, representing the elements in the community with which it must maintain a live relationship if it is to do its job.

Firstly, it must establish its identity and its functions in relation to other organisations. A Family Service Unit, for example, although a voluntary agency, may depend on the Health and Children's Committees of the Local Authority for much of its income, and on a variety of agencies for referrals. No small part of the work of the Unit Leader is to secure for the Unit an established position in relation to the constellation of agencies as one of which it offers its services.

Secondly, an agency must establish its identity in relation to clients – actual and potential. Traditionally, the statutory social services have been 'crisis centred', either imposing themselves on clients, or being resorted to for help in crisis situations, and being used mainly by the 'lower income' and 'underprivileged' sections of the community. The concept of 'prevention' demands a different basis for contact: a Family Advice Centre will be fully effective only if it becomes widely known and accepted as a place where people seek early help of their own accord – as some have already learned to use the 'kindred social work' service of the Probation Officer.

Thirdly, an agency's identity needs to be established in the community. Children's Departments depend on the community for foster parents; the Probation and Aftercare Service plans to make use of volunteers; voluntary agencies call on the community for financial support; the concept of 'community care' calls for community understanding of the needs of the mentally ill, the deprived child, the old, discharged prisoners, the unmarried mother, and of the services which social work agencies can make available to them.

These three examples indicate the scope, and the need, for the Executive to act as public relations officer for his agency. As community organisation gains increasing recognition as a social work method, so will additional importance attach to the Executive's task of interpreting the agency to the community.

2. THE SKILLS OF THE SOCIAL WORK ADMINISTRATOR

A range of diverse but interrelated tasks has been identified for the Executive, and for those who participate with him in the administration of social work agencies. It may be well in conclusion to suggest the types of skills upon which the performance of these tasks will draw.

First and foremost, administration calls for skill in working with people. Enough it is hoped has been said throughout this book to make it clear that social work administration is a process implemented by people, through people, and for people; and with all the limitations which the organisational setting places on the satisfaction of individual needs, it is nevertheless with the promotion of the human purposes of the agency that the social work administrator is primarily concerned. One writer has suggested that the social work administrator works with four different sets of relationship. He has a 'one-to-one' working relationship with individual members of staff; he works with a small group system, as with his committee, his staff as a whole, or groups within the total staff; he works with a complex organisation as he administers the agency as a total social system; and he must develop relationships which extend beyond the agency itself into the community. A parallel may be apparent with the social work methods of casework, groupwork, and community organisation. The position, roles, and functions of the administrator are not those of the social worker, and it would be unwise to carry the analogy too far. But if skill in working with a variety of human relationships is something which the social worker seeks consciously to develop in his function with clients, it is no less appropriate to the administrator in working with the agency.

Secondly, administration calls for specific technical skills, which the knowledge and skills of the social worker cannot supplant. Fundamentally, the social worker's social science knowledge about inter-personal and group relationships must be supplemented by an understanding of the nature of organisations, and by skill in working within an organisational context. More specifically, an Executive needs in various way to be his agency's 'expert': on the law related to the agency's function, on committee procedure, in the techniques of working with a committee, and in the use of tools of financial control, such as the budget. He must understand and utilise supervision as essentially an administrative process, and have sufficient knowledge about current social work practice to appreciate how it should be developed. He needs too a sufficiently clear understanding of his own administrative function to recognise the proper boundary between it and the function of the specialists who provide the agency's social work service.

A third suggestion comes from Helen Montgomery (1962), who proposes that the administrator also needs 'conceptual' skills: the ability to 'see the agency whole'; to conceive of it within a context of past and future, with the potentiality for change and growth; to conceptualise the implications of particular pieces of action; to be able to identify and correct errors 'whether in philosophy or procedure, at their point of origin, and not at the end of the assembly line'.

It is perhaps through the development of 'conceptual' skills that the administrator can most effectively begin to make of administration a truly creative activity.

Conclusion

The hypothesis underlying all that has been said so far is that administration, creatively and skilfully used, is a process whereby social work agencies may become more effective instruments for providing a service to clients. Administration has been presented as a method with its own content and skills, which the administrator may learn to use, as the social worker learns to use the knowledge and skills appropriate to the practice of social work. Yet another assertion has been that a beginning has hardly as yet been made in the application to agency administration of the social science theory upon which social workers draw in their work with clients.

There have however during the last few years been tangible signs of a stirring interest. The U.N. Seminar on 'The Training of Senior Personnel for the Social Services' held in the Netherlands in 1963, analysed the functions of senior personnel, and discussed desirable developments in their training (U.N., 1963). The Association of Social Workers in 1965 sponsored a study conference on 'New Thinking about Administration'. A Home Office short course on staff supervision for senior staff in Children's Departments, held at Leicester in the same year, revealed a very active concern and interest on the part of course members in their role not simply as social work supervisors, but as administrators. The Association of Child Care Officers following a resolution of its Annual General Meeting in 1965, is pressing for full time training courses in administration. Teaching on organisations is being introduced into some Applied Social Studies courses. And the London School of Economics in 1966 offers opportunities for one year's full time study, to trained and experienced social workers, including those entering senior administrative posts.

In an address to the Royal Society of Health (Guardian, 1965), Professor Titmuss has suggested that the problem of the shortage of trained social workers in the Local Authority social work services might in part at least be tackled not simply by increased recruitment, but by the more effective deployment and use of existing personnel, within a reformed administrative structure. A recent book by Professor Donnison (1965) and his colleagues explores the implications, for the implementation of social policy, of the 'local level' administration of social agencies. Traditionally, the academic discipline known as 'Social Policy and Administration' has been concerned with the study of the development, functions, and structure of the social services, rather than with the nature of the administrative processes through which social policy is implemented in social work agencies themselves; but the two above examples may be symptomatic of a new orientation. We may be reaching the stage at which it would be useful to distinguish between the two disciplines of 'Social Policy and Administration', and 'Social Work Administration' : that is the study of the internal processes through which social work agencies are managed. The two are interrelated to the extent that the administrator has a function in relation to the formulation and implementation of social policy (as Professor Donnison's book well illustrates); but they are distinct to the extent that this is but one aspect of the total administrative process.

The clarification of administration as a distinct area of study in relation to social work can be justified, however, only if the application of theories of administration would seem to have a contribution to make to the more effective functioning of social work agencies. It may therefore be appropriate to identify some aspects of the existing situation, the restructuring of the statutory social work services apart, which indicate the existence of problems which are administrative in character.

Firstly, there is within the statutory social work services a trend towards larger and more complex organisational units, which would be intensified if even the social services for children were restructured. Children's Departments already offer an example of this trend. They have since 1948 been given additional statutory functions, and partly in order that their 'preventive' services may be within easier reach of potential clients, but also because of population growth and movement, they are tending to decentralise. The Curtis Committee envisaged that the Children's Officer would be in direct personal contact with children in care (Home Department, 1946); but now there may be several layers in the hierarchy between the Children's Officer and the agency's clients. His function is not to be a social worker, but to administer a complex organisation. A comparable situation may exist in the Probation Service, with the combining of Probation Areas, and the opening of area offices. As agencies grow in size and complexity, their 'top level' administration calls for the practice of administrative rather than social work skills.

Secondly, the expansion of agencies calls for *more* administrators – in the 'middle management' layer. The current practice is for these to be recruited from amongst social workers, who as such are in universally short supply, and many of whom, it may be hazarded, move into administrative positions not because they want to be administrators, but because this is the only channel of promotion available to them. If this is so, then there are major problems in relation to a career structure. Is there perhaps a need for a channel of promotion through a hierarchy of social work positions, so that people who want to continue to practise social work, and whose training and skills are in social work, may not be propelled into work which is less congenial to them, and for which they have no special qualifications? If this is so, then there are problems to be faced concerning the distribution of administrative and social work functions within agencies: how are senior 'social work' positions to be differentiated from 'administrative' ones? An alternative, or parallel, question relates to what is certainly a widespread lack of appreciation of the potential interest and scope of the administrator's job. If administration were understood as a dynamic and creative activity, rather than a static and routine one, might more administrators find increasing satisfaction in their jobs, and more potential administrators come to light?

Such questions as these give rise to further questions about the future recruitment of social work administrators. Need those who hold senior administrative positions in social work agencies themselves be fully qualified and experienced social workers? Or is it enough that they should have sufficient knowledge about current social work practice, and sufficient sympathy with it, to be able to provide the agency's social workers with the organisational support they need? This is a complicated question, but it may need attention if recruits to the social services are not to be expensively trained for social work; and then subsequently be 'drained off' to become untrained administrators.

Further to recruitment are questions relating to training. Firstly, is training needed? And if so, what forms might it take, and at what stage in an individual's career could it most usefully be made available to him? Furthermore, although students on professional social work courses are training to be social workers and not administrators, might it be appropriate to introduce them at this stage to the idea of social work administration, and to give them the opportunity of considering the nature of the organisations of which they as social workers will be a part; the contribution which good administration can make to an agency; and in particular, the nature of their own administrative responsibilities as agency employees? Questions will then need to be asked about what it is that the administrator as such needs to know and be able to do; and what social workers need to know and be able to do in their capacities as members of a working administrative unit (Council on Social Work Education, 1959).

In this concluding section, a variety of issues have been presented in the form of questions, for two reasons. Firstly, there may be no general agreement that these are in fact important issues, for they have not so far been very widely explored. Secondly, in so far as the issues themselves may be accepted as being relevant, it is certain that there are as yet no answers. But these may be questions of a kind which, in the present state of concern about the staffing of the social services, call for consideration within agencies, by professional social work associations, and by those who are at points at which the nature of the problems which have here been tentatively indicated can be more precisely identified.

Developments in social legislation make ever-increasing demands on social work, and it seems improbable that there will ever be enough social workers to go round. But what is 'enough'? If it is unrealistic to expect that all social work vacancies will ever be filled, it is also inappropriate to look on the recruitment of additional social workers as the only way of increasing the amount and quality of social work service available. It may be that with our splintered social service structure, and tardy attention to problems of administration, some of the professional manpower we already have is being wasted (Jefferys, 1965), and that there is much that remains to be done to free existing social workers, within their own agencies, to use their abilities to the full.

Suggestions for further reading

There is an almost complete lack of literature in this country on administration as it applies specifically to social work agencies, and thus the reader is likely to have to do some translating for himself. He may, for example, have to consider how theories about organisations can be applied to social work agencies; and how far material on social work administration in the United States is relevant to agencies in Great Britain. The following suggestions are made with these provisos in mind. The bibliographical references given in the text will also provide a guide to reading on specific points.

1. *Dynamic Administration* (Metcalf (ed.) 1941). The papers of Mary Follett are a stimulating presentation of the principles which the author believed to be integral to sound administration. Although the papers were addressed to industrialists, the psychological and philosophical ideas which they explore are relevant to administration in any setting.

2. *Modern Organisations* (Etzioni, 1964) is a precise and lucid account by a sociologist of the development of theories about the nature of organisations. It contains a particularly useful section on 'Administrative and Professional Author-

ity', with some specific reference to social work agencies.

3. *Bureaucracy in Modern Society* (Blau, 1963) is an illuminating guide to the characteristics of bureaucracy, and discusses its implications for democratic administration. 'Positive' as well as negative aspects are usefully discussed.

4. *Social Policy and Administration* (Donnison, 1965) is an invaluable analysis of the significance of local administration for the implementation of social policy.

5. *Social Welfare Administration* (Reed (ed.) 1961) is a collection of papers designed to introduce some 'current concepts, responsibilities, and trends in administration', and if due allowance is made for the American 'setting', it provides a useful discussion of the 'generic' and 'special' elements in administration as it applies to social work agencies.

6. *Administrative Behaviour* (Simon, 1961) is an indispensable interpretation of the nature of administration, which the author sees primarily in terms of decision-making. The chapter on 'authority' provides a useful example of a concept which while familiar to social workers, has a different connotation in an administrative context.

7. The forthcoming monograph in this series, *The Student and Supervision in Social Work Education* (Young, P.H.F.), is recommended for an analysis of the supervisory process within the overall context of the agency as an organisation, and of the supervisor's role as an administrator.

8. *Writers on Organisations* (Pugh, 1964). Sponsored by the Administrative Staff College at Henley, this is a 'guide book' to the ideas of major writers on organisations. It offers material on the structure of organisations, their functioning, their management, people in organisations, and the organisation in society. It provides a concise but comprehensive introduction to organisation theory; but as the authors assert that 'theory and practice are inseparable', the book has also a direct practical quality.

Bibliography

ARGYRIS, C. (1964) *Integrating the Individual and the Organization*,
New York: Wiley.

BARNARD, C. (1938) *The Functions of the Executive*,
Harvard University Press (reprinted 1950).

BLAU, P. M. (1963) *Bureaucracy in Modern Society*,
New York: Random House.

BLAU, P. M. and SCOTT, R. W. (1963) *Formal Organizations*,
London: Routledge and Kegan Paul.

BLAU, P. M. (1963) *The Dynamics of Bureaucracy*,
University of Chicago.

BOURDILLON, A. F. C. (ed.) (1945) *Voluntary Social Services*,
London: Methuen.

BROWN, W. (1960) *Exploration in Management*,
London: Heinemann.

CASE CONFERENCE (1965) Advertisement, Vol. XII, November.

CHILDREN ACT, 1948.

COUNCIL ON SOCIAL WORK EDUCATION (1959) *Social Work
Curriculum Study*, Vol. XII, New York: Columbia University Press.

DONNISON, D. V. and CHAPMAN, V. (1965) *Social Policy and
Administration*, London: Allen and Unwin.

DONNISON, D. V. and STUART, M. (1958) *The Child and the Social
Services*, London: Fabian Society.

ETZIONI, A. (1961) *A Comparative Analysis of Complex
Organizations*, Glencoe: Free Press.

ETZIONI, A. (1964) *Modern Organizations*,
New Jersey: Prentice Hall.

GERTH, H. H. and MILLS, C. W. (1948) *From Max Weber; Essays in
Sociology*, London: Routledge and Kegan Paul (reprinted 1961).

GOFFMAN, E. (1961), *Asylums*,
New York: Doubleday.

GOULDNER, A. W. (1955), *Patterns of Industrial Bureaucracy*,
London: Routledge and Kegan Paul.

GUARDIAN (1965), March 26th.

HOME DEPARTMENT, MINISTRY OF EDUCATION, AND MINISTRY
OF HEALTH (1946) *Report of the Care of Children Committee*
(Curtis Report), London: H.M.S.O.

HOME OFFICE (1962) *Report of the Departmental Committee on the
Probation Service* (Morison Report), London: H.M.S.O.

HOME OFFICE (1965), *The Child, the Family, and the Young
Offender*, London: H.M.S.O.

JEFFERYS, M. (1965) *An Anatomy of Social Welfare Services*,
London: Michael Joseph.

JOHNS, R. (1963) *Confronting Organizational Change*,
New York: Association Press.

KAMMERER, G. M. (1962) *British and American Child Welfare
Services*, Detroit: Wayne State University Press.

LINTON, R. (1963) 'Status and Role', *Sociological Theory*,
Coser, L. A., and Rosenberg, B., New York: Macmillan.

LIPPITT, R., *et al.* (1958) *The Dynamics of Planned Change*,
New York: Harcourt Brace.

LUPTON, T. (1964) *Industrial Behaviour and Personnel Management*,
London: Institute of Personnel Management.

MANNHEIM, K. (1954) *Ideology and Utopia*,
London: Routledge and Kegan Paul.

MCGREGOR, D. (1960) *The Human side of Enterprise*,
New York: McGraw Hill.

MAYO, E. (1946) *The Human Problems of Industrial Civilization*,
Harvard University Press.

METCALF, H. C. and URWICK, L. (eds.) (1941), *Dynamic
Administration*, Bath: Management Publications Trust.

MONTGOMERY, H. (1962) 'The Practice of Administration'
Child Welfare, Vol. XI, No. 2.

MOORE, W. E. (1963) *Social Change*,
New Jersey: Prentice Hall.

MORGAN, R. (1962) 'Role Performance in a Bureaucracy',
Social Work Practice, New York: National Conference on Social
Welfare.

OSBORN, P. (1958) 'National Assistance in Great Britain',
Social Service Review, Vol. XXXII, September.

OWEN, R. (1813) *A New View of Society*,
London: Dent (reprinted 1949).

PARSONS, T. (1960) *Structure and Process in Modern Societies*,
Glencoe: Free Press.

PUGH, D. S., *et al.* (1964) *Writers on Organisations*,
London: Hutchinson.

BIBLIOGRAPHY

REED, E. (ed.) (1961) *Social Welfare Administration*,
New York: Columbia University Press.
RICE, A. K. (1963) *The Enterprise and its Environment*,
London: Tavistock Publications.
RICHMOND, M. (1917) *Social Diagnosis*,
New York: Russell Sage Foundation (reprinted 1955).
ROETHLISBERGER, F. J. (1955) *Management and Morale*,
Harvard University Press.
SELZNICK, P. (1964) 'Foundations of a Theory of Organisation',
Complex Organisations: a Sociological Reader, Etzioni, A.,
New York: Holt Rinehart.
SELZNICK, P. (1957) *Leadership in Administration*,
New York: Rowe Peterson & Co.
SIMON, H. A. (1961) *Administrative Behaviour*,
New York: Macmillan (2nd ed.).
SUMNER, W. (1906) *Folkways*,
Boston: Ginn & Co. (reprinted 1959).
TAWNEY, R. H. (1926) *Religion and the Rise of Capitalism*,
London: Penguin Books (reprinted 1964).
THOMPSON, J. D. and MCEWEN, W. (1964) 'Organisational Goals and
Environment', *Complex Organisations: a Sociological Reader*.
Etzioni, A., New York: Holt Rinehart.
TIMMS, N. (1962) *Casework in the Child Care Service*,
London: Butterworth.
TITMUSS, R. (1958) *Essays on the Welfare State*,
London: Allen and Unwin.
UNITED NATIONS (1963) *Training of Senior Personnel for the Social
Services*, Geneva: United Nations.
URWICK, L. and BRECH, E. F. L. (1951) *The Making of Scientific
Management*, London: Pitman.
WEBER, M. (1958) *The Protestant Ethic and the Spirit of Capitalism*,
English translation, New York: Scribners.
WINNICOTT, C. (1964) 'Casework and Agency Function', *Child
Care and Social Work*, London: Codicote Press.